EXPERT SYSTEMS AND CASE LAW

ELLIS HORWOOD BOOKS IN INFORMATION TECHNOLOGY

General Editor: Professor V. A. J. MALLER, ICL Chair in Computer Systems, Loughborough University of Technology; formerly of Thorn EMI Information Technology Ltd
Consulting Editors: Dr JOHN M. M. PINKERTON, Information Technology Consultant, J & H Pinkerton Associates, Esher, Surrey, and formerly Manager Strategic Requirements, International Computers Limited; and PATRICK HOLLIGAN, Department of Computer Studies, Loughborough University of Technology

EXPERT SYSTEMS AND CASE LAW

URI J. SCHILD Ph.D.
Department of Mathematics and Computer Science
Bar Ilan University, Israel

ELLIS HORWOOD
NEW YORK   LONDON   TORONTO   SYDNEY   TOKYO   SINGAPORE

First published in 1992 by
ELLIS HORWOOD LIMITED
Market Cross House, Cooper Street,
Chichester, West Sussex, PO19 1EB, England

A division of
Simon & Schuster International Group
A Paramount Communications Company

Printed and bound in Great Britain
by Bookcraft Ltd, Midsomer Norton, Avon

British Library Cataloguing-in-Publication Data

Schild, Uri J.
Expert systems and case law. —
(Ellis Horwood series in information technology)
I. Title. II. Series
006.3026
ISBN 0–13–048463–6

Library of Congress Cataloging-in-Publication Data available

Contents

---

¹ Only sections and subsections (1.6, 1.6.2, 1.6.3, etc.) are listed. Subsubsections (1.6.3.1, etc.) are not listed. More detailed information may be sought in the *Index*.

PART TWO. Related Work: Factual Description and Critique.

Chapter Three: Related Work.

Chapter Four: Discussion of Related Work.

My thanks to Marek Sergot, who was my thesis supervisor. Despite his involvement in numerous activities he always found time to listen to me and part-take in many fruitful discussions. The book is dedicated to my wife, Rivka. I admire her infinite patience and thank her for the encouragement she has given me.

Preface

It often happens that a certain word which is used to describe a particular concept changes its meaning. It is applied out of context and used erroneously by people with the best of intentions. 'Expert Systems' is such a word-combination. It is used indiscriminately for all kinds of computer systems, which are not representative of the original concept. In Britain the concept of '(Intelligent) Knowledge Based Systems' has been introduced to alleviate the problem. However, one cannot say that this or indeed any other concept has met with universal approval. For that reason we have used 'Expert Systems' in the title of this book and in some other places. This has not been done without misgivings, and in the majority of places we simply refer to 'computer systems' for case-law.

The greater part of the work was carried out while I was a member of the Logic Programming Group at Imperial College, London. I have therefore used English (as contrasted with American) spelling throughout the book, e.g. neighbour and not: neighbor. If, nevertheless, my attempts at consistency have not been entirely successful, I hereby apologize (apologise?).

The book grew out of my Ph.D. thesis and some later work. My major aim has been to examine the possibility of building *practical* computer systems for case-law and other domains where human discretionary judgment is called for. To that end we consider existing case-law systems (prototypes) and describe two of our own systems. We contend that the latter could be developed into program products for commercial applications.

Most publications in the area of Artificial Intelligence and Law have so far been found in a small number of monographs and in the proceedings of conferences such as ICAIL (International Conference on Artificial Intelligence and Law: 1987, 1989, 1991) and the Florence conferences organised by IDG (Istituto per la Documentazione Giuridica). We have attempted to include references and descriptions of recent work from all the above sources including ICAIL-91.

The first of our own systems to be described is called **JURIX**, perhaps to be interpreted as a contraction of the words 'Jurisprudence' and 'Expert'. The name **JURIX** was first applied to our system in June 1988 (see [Schild88]). It has since been used for a series of annual conferences in Holland beginning in December 1988. The second system is called Meta, as it creates and applies meta-rules in the legal domain.

PART ONE

Legal Systems: Fundamental Concepts

1

Introduction

Cox and Box appeared in court.
After Cox had presented his argument
the judge said: "You are right".
Then Box presented his side, and
the judge said: "You too are right!"
"Your Honour", said the clerk,
"they cannot both be right".
Said the judge: "You are also right -
Damn these open textured concepts".

(Deciphered from Hammurabi's stone)

1.1 The Basic Problem.

The problems which we shall consider in this book relate to the building of a legal expert system. Such a system would carry out an analysis given the facts of a legal situation or propose a plan of action in accordance with the applicable body of statutory law and collection of relevant precedents from prior court decisions. The system would have an advisory function and be built with a lawyer, a judge or an adjudicating clerk as its primary user. The possibility of a layman using such a system (D-I-Y law?) seems impractical, as we shall see later; the idea may even seem heretical to persons with a formal legal education.

Our aim is specifically to consider problems that arise with computer-based systems for *case-law*, i.e., law based (perhaps exclusively) upon decisions handed down in previous cases. When a new case comes to court a decision will be made by the judge using previous cases (precedents) in one of several ways. For the moment it suffices to say that the judge will consider the application of a precedent if it exhibits some kind of similarity to the case at hand.

Compared with the amount of work carried out in the area of computer-based systems for statutory law, relatively few researchers have addressed the problems in the area of case-law systems. In this book we shall discuss the problems involved and attempt to understand the reasons why this area so far has been largely unexplored. We shall discuss previous approaches to the solution of the problems and propose some ideas of our own towards their solution.

When attempting to build a legal computer system for case-law a central issue one must deal with involves the concept of legal reasoning: As already mentioned above, we have to clarify how a judge applies precedents to a new case in order to reach a decision.

Among the various activities in legal reasoning we shall identify two: (i) The process for establishing facts and (ii) The search for applicable regulations and other sources. We shall now explain why the first activity will only be considered briefly in this work, while the latter is of major interest for us.

Some areas of law, e.g. criminal law, are strongly dependent on the first kind of reasoning, involving all the complexities of daily life: Human actions, beliefs, intentions, motivations etc. In other areas, e.g. commercial and corporate law, the facts are commonly clear-cut and unambiguous. On the other hand, concepts and legislation in these latter areas have deep technical complexity. Human beings may have difficulty in grasping this complexity, however, and this is precisely why some have argued that such areas are particularly suited for computer applications ([McCarty80]). Areas like Torts and Contracts occupy an intermediate position. There is usually not a central dependency on the acceptance of certain facts. One does not hear speeches in court like the following: "Members of the Jury, no less than three witnesses saw the accused leave the premises at exactly eight o'clock with a blood-stained knife in his hand - and yet he asserts that he was out of town all week." On the other hand, the facts do not exhibit the same complexity as found in, e.g., cases dealing with stock transactions. This may be the reason why these subjects are usually taught in first year law-school. Yet, when choosing one of these particular fields for implementation of a legal computer system, there is still a need to confront problems of common-sense knowledge and speech-understanding. It can then happen that the effort needed to deal with these aspects dominates and diverts the attention from other problems of legal reasoning.

It is important to understand that a user is only seldom asking a question like: "Do the facts at hand represent a tort?", but rather asks: "Do the facts at hand *suffice* to obtain a decision in court for a tort?". The two kinds of legal reasoning mentioned above are therefore not really separate, but interact when one attempts to deal with practical problems. We shall keep this observation in mind later, when we shall discuss the choice of an appropriate area of law for our studies.

The question of which facts may be proven and will suffice in court is not always touched upon in textbooks of law. Nevertheless, this is a problem every practicing lawyer must deal with when undertaking litigation. In fact, one could perhaps attempt to extract the expertise on this subject from lawyers who appear often and successfully in court, and build an expert system of what we shall call the 'classical' type.

An expert system of this type may be described as "a knowledge-intensive program that solves problems normally requiring human expertise" ([Hayes-Roth84]). Most expert systems consist of (1) a set of facts describing a particular problem domain and (2) a set of assertions or inference rules defining relationships between the facts and specifying how new facts can be deduced from existing facts by means of the assertions. Taken together, the facts and assertions, which are elicited from a *human expert*, form a "knowledge-base". Inferences are made in accordance with a particular control strategy that is defined separately and independently from the knowledge about the problem domain. Many expert systems provide for facts and rules with associated probabilities or certainty factors, in order to handle uncertainty in data and knowledge. For further definitions and descriptions of this type of expert system see e.g. [Hayes-Roth83].

Susskind in [Susskind87] calls this kind of expert system in the legal field an 'experiential' system. Such a system could perhaps also incorporate knowledge relating to skills of argumentation and rhetoric. However, our main interest in this book is in computer-systems that aim to represent the law *itself*, and not an expert's own interpretation of how the legal system works in a particular area of law. Such a system has been called an 'academic' system by Susskind.

Before actually considering the problems involved in building legal computer systems for case-law we shall discuss a certain line of argumentation which possibly may be taken by persons lacking a proper legal background and knowledge. Such a person could argue that it is natural to apply computers to problems of law, more - perhaps - than to many other subjects, as law and legislation are intended to be precise formulations of requirements and are therefore commonly (but erroneously) considered consistent and unambiguous. Indeed, such a party may proceed to assert, the field of legal information retrieval appears to be well-developed, judging from the fact that commercial systems are marketed and utilized by the legal profession. One might therefore (again erroneously) conclude that the building of legal systems for case-law is an easy task to carry out.

We shall see below how law has an intrinsic feature of vagueness which makes building legal computer systems an extremely complex undertaking. A major aim of this book is to consider how to deal with this vagueness.

Concerning legal information retrieval systems we shall briefly define this concept and devote some remarks to it. Consider first a general definition of this area:

"Information Retrieval is concerned with the representation, storage, organization and accessing of information items" ([Salton83], p. 10).

This general definition can be applied to the particular domain of law. A *legal* information retrieval system operates on a database consisting of *legal* items. These items may be of different kinds, e.g. contracts, testaments, research articles on legal topics, etc. From our point of view the main items of interest are texts of statutory law and case-reports. In response to a request by a user the system will extract individual pieces of relevant texts from the database. In the existing commercial systems this retrieval is usually carried out by searching the texts for the appearance of certain keywords (or combinations of keywords) supplied by the user. It is a question how much these systems are used and how useful they are, as is exemplified by the following quotation by a leading researcher in the field: "A need clearly exists for systems that move beyond text-searching to systems based on the meaning and legal significance of documents" ([Hafner87]). A survey of such "classical" retrieval systems in law is given by [Kauffman87]. In a later chapter we shall consider some modern approaches to legal retrieval systems which use methods of 'conceptual retrieval' and their relevance to our problem.

In the field of legal expert systems we shall see that many large and challenging problems must be solved before it will be possible to reach a level similar to the one attained in the area of legal information systems. In this book we shall describe some of these problems and various approaches to their solution. We shall explain why our approach will be to create a system for *advice* and *support* of the human user, and not a system which gives definite answers. Specifically, we shall describe two systems, **JURIX** and Meta, developed by us. These systems illustrate two types of advisory systems intended as a help for a human user engaged in legal reasoning.

1.2 The Anglo-American Legal System.

In the previous section we stated that the search for applicable regulations is one of the central issues of a legal computer system. This search will depend on the legal system in force, which may differ from one country to another. We shall briefly summarize the system which is in force not only in England, but also in Scotland (partly), Ireland, The British Dominions and the United States of America.

The primary sources consist (mostly) of two parts: statutory law and case-law. In this book we shall mainly be concerned with case-law. Historically case-law evolved from *common-law*, the collection of laws "common" in early times to the whole Kingdom of England. It was held together by the doctrine of *stare decisis*, or standing by previous decisions. Thus when a judge decided a new problem in a case brought before him, this became a new rule of law to be followed by subsequent judges. It is of course far from obvious how this is to be done, for a given case may be related to several previous cases with conflicting decisions. In later times the stare decisis crystallized into the form which is known today as the doctrine of judicial precedent, which will be explained below.

The doctrine of judicial precedent distinguishes between two kinds of precedents: binding precedents, that judges are bound to follow, and precedents which are merely persuasive. The application depends upon an accurate record being kept of previous decisions, as has indeed been the case for centuries in all the countries where the English legal system applies. Such *law-reports* attempt to state the *ratio decidendi*, i.e. the principle on which the case is decided. However, it is very seldom that the judge states the ratio decidendi in explicit and precise terms, so the ratio decidendi of a precedent may be narrowed or widened by a subsequent judge before whom the case is cited as an authority. Thus the eventual and accepted ratio decidendi of a case may not be the ratio decidendi that the judge who decided the case would himself have chosen, but the one which has been approved by subsequent judges. This is inevitable, because a judge, when deciding a case will give his reasons but will not usually distinguish in his remarks in any rigid or immutable way, between what we have called the ratio decidendi, and what are called *obiter dicta*. The latter are things said in passing, and they do not have binding force, but may yet have some persuasive power.

While decisions made in higher courts are binding precedents, decisions made in lower courts and decisions from other countries using the English legal system are considered as persuasive precedents only.

Legal areas where statutory laws have been enacted may also include case-law. Statutory law is inherently vague and often ambiguous. It therefore needs to be interpreted by the courts. This gives rise to case-law, for decisions reached by the courts in their interpretation of the legislation are binding according to the rules stated above.

1.3 Relevance to Other Fields.

1.3.1 Other Legal Systems.

Besides the common-law tradition described in the previous section there are two additional legal traditions in the contemporary world: civil law and socialist law.

In addition to statutes and administrative regulations the civil law tradition commonly recognizes a third source of law called custom (see [Merryman85]). It is assumed that whatever the problem before the judge, he will always be able to find some form of law to apply - whether a statute, a regulation or an applicable custom.

This dogmatic conception of law as being composed exclusively of statutes, regulations and customs holds in theory only. Previous decisions have as a practical matter considerable influence upon the future judicial handling of comparable situations. Courts which have made the decisions in the past retain full freedom to decide in a different way in similar cases that they will be called upon to decide in the future. But, in fact, these reversals hardly ever take place and the precedents, if they do not bind the judges, inevitably inspire them (see [vonMehren77]).

The effect of the communistic legal reform in Russia and afterwards in the other socialistic countries was to impose certain principles of socialistic ideology on the existing civil law systems. Decisions have a considerable influence on future similar cases also in countries following this legal tradition ([Merryman85]).

1.3.2 Quasi-Legal Areas.

The area of law makes a formal use of precedents and rulings in the judicial decision-making process. There are other areas where decision-making takes place according to specified regulations and provisions and where an informal use is often made of previous examples and conclusions.

There are many examples of such domains. In certain areas, like the Social Services, officials, who often have no legal qualification, administer laws and make legal decisions based on precedents. We shall refer to such officials as adjudicating clerks. In many large companies internal regulations relating to employee benefits, pension-plans etc. are applied by clerks who also consider previous, similar cases. In educational institutions decisions involving acceptance of students, authorizing their study-programs, etc. are based on rules and use precedents. In all these circumstances the decision process is usually quite uncomplicated. However, there are cases where conflicting arguments may be put forward. The decision process then involves the weighing of ambiguous and contradictory evidence arising from previous examples, and eventually it calls for a human discretionary judgment.

We shall call domains of the above type: quasi-legal areas. In all such areas the adjudicating clerk will presumably attempt to make a decision which seems fair to him. However, as formal records are not kept there is no uniformity in decisions made by different officials or even among decisions made by the same official at different times. Even if precedents are recorded the adjudicating clerks almost never state the exact reasons for their decisions in a formal manner.

It therefore seems that a certain amount of arbitrariness may be involved in quasi-legal procedures. On the other hand, in none of the above areas would it seem possible to maintain the kind of machinery that one finds in actual legal domains, viz. legally educated personnel, binding judicial precedence and law-reports.

One may therefore assume that computer systems for decision support in quasi-legal areas could be of even greater practical importance than in proper legal domains. The system Meta, which we shall describe in chapter six, has been implemented in a quasi-legal area.

1.4 What is a Legal Expert System?

In section 1.1 we briefly introduced the notion of an expert system. We shall now make some further observations relating to legal expert systems. This will serve to introduce some factual knowledge concerning such systems and will also indicate the precise scope of the present work.

Consider the following characterization of what we have previously called a 'classical' expert system (adapted from [Hayes-Roth83]): An expert system is a man-machine system with specialized problem-solving expertise. The expertise consists of knowledge about a particular domain, understanding of domain problems, and skill at solving some of these problems. To this definition one usually adds the requirement that the system must have the capability of explaining its line of reasoning and conclusions.

Several observations can be made in connection with this characterization.

1. Problem solving in the general sense has always had a central role in the field of Artificial Intelligence. Much work has been carried out, mainly - but not exclusively - using search methods. One can, e.g. consider the GPS (General Problem Solver) program ([Ernst69]). This program was intended to model human performance in (search) problems such as puzzles, games and symbolic integration. Today the concept of problem solving has changed somewhat, and has taken on the domain-dependent sense used for expert systems. This is of course also the sense we use in this work.

2. One of the reasons for introducing the name "expert system" was probably in order to indicate that one or more human experts cooperate in formulating and introducing their expert knowledge to the computer. Its use in the legal field (and perhaps in other fields too) is somewhat unfortunate. It may lead to the erroneous impression that the computer is the 'expert' and as such may substitute in *all* roles of a human expert. Thus the possibility of appointing a computerized legal expert system to the bench may seem a real one, as has indeed been proposed and discussed more than once (see [Gardner87], p.79-83 for a survey of this subject).

One may indeed envisage a system which an individual may query whether or not the requirements of certain statutes and regulations (or rather their computer formalization) seem to be fulfilled in an actual or hypothetical case. As an example of such use one may take the formalization of the British Nationality Act, to be surveyed below, in chapter 3. An individual may be interested to know whether or not he is a citizen. A query to the system would indicate the provisions of the Act which apply in his particular circumstances, and what the outcome of their application would be. Similarly the TAXMAN I system also described in more detail below, may be used to analyse the tax consequences of certain corporate reorganizations under the United States Internal Revenue Code.

However, most people, including computer scientists, agree that legal decision making should be an exclusively human enterprise. In all but trivial administrative situations judgments should *not* be made by a computer. However, it seems perfectly natural to employ a system that would be a decision-making *aid* to an individual. It is therefore perhaps more appropriate to use the name: "legal advisory system" or "legal decision support system" in such a case, which would still come under the general definition given above.

3. The requirements of such a legal advisory system have been discussed by L. Thorne McCarty in two papers, [McCarty80a] and [McCarty82a]. He distinguishes three kinds of systems: Legal Retrieval Systems, Legal Analysis Systems and Legal Planning Systems. [Hafner87] presents the state of the art in the area of intelligent document retrieval systems, which we shall not discuss further at this point but take up again in chapter three. A legal analysis or planning system: "would analyse a set of facts, or propose a sequence of transactions in accordance with the applicable body of legal rules" ([McCarty80a]). A system developed for the purposes of legal analysis may also be used for the purpose of legal planning. In the former case the system would deal with factual data, while in the latter case it would be presented with hypothetical data. The sense of "planning" as used here differs of course from the one often used in AI applications, where, e.g. robots generate and carry out plans of action (see [Charniak85], chapter nine).

4. Our approach will differ from the one exemplified by LDS, an expert system in the area of settling claims in product liability cases, and developed by Waterman and Peterson (see [Waterman80], [Waterman81]). LDS is constructed in the programming language ROSIE and attempts to model how such claims are settled in practice out of court. The aim was thus not to determine whether liability exists but to simulate the behaviour of lawyers and claims adjusters. LDS represents an expert system in the classical style of MYCIN ([Shortliffe76]) and PROSPECTOR ([Duda80]), where the particular knowledge of each system was obtained by elicitation from human experts.

Another system of somewhat similar kind is TAXADVISOR (see [Michaelsen82], [Michaelsen84]). This system is implemented using EMYCIN. It was developed for the purpose of assisting lawyers with tax-planning for their clients. The knowledge-base contains the kind of expert knowledge that is used by (human) tax-advisors. It does not attempt to represent the law itself.

In section 1.1 we referred to this kind of expert system as an 'experiential' system. Knowledge about what facts can be established in court and how to present arguments in court may be elicited from an expert lawyer and incorporated in a system of the same type as LDS. It seems highly probable that such a system should be domain-specific, i.e., one such system should be built for tort-cases, one for contract-cases etc. For the expert knowledge specific to tort-cases may only partly overlap with the expert knowledge specific to contract cases etc. It is conceivable that the domain must be narrowed even further down, so one would develop a system specifically for negligence, etc. This type of expert system could also incorporate concepts from probability theory and (given the appropriate statistics) advise a client about his chances for winning his case in court.

Several systems of the experiential kind have been developed. Most of them are prototype systems or working models, and it is difficult to determine to what extent they have had actual application. We shall here mention one real applicable system which is the first commercially available expert system in Law in the U.K. This system, The Latent Damage System, was developed by P.N. Capper (the domain expert) and R. Susskind (see [Capper88] and [Susskind89]). It addresses: "the difficult legal issues relating to the time periods within which claimants may start proceedings in the law of negligence if the damage or loss suffered was latent (that is discovered some time after its occurrence)" ([Susskind89], p.24).

This system is an experiential system in the sense defined by Susskind himself. As he states in [Susskind89a]:

"There never was any intention of directly translating the Latent Damage Act 1986 into some computer formalism: the goal, rather, was to implement in a system a leading expert's conception and interpretation of the Act and related law" ([Susskind89a], p.598).

The system is intended for lawyers and for other advisers in professional practice. Despite the above quotation it differs in nature from both of the other systems with respect to the depth of its knowledge and its jurisprudential approach, as: "it will guide a user through all and only those legal rules that bear on the problem at hand" ([Susskind89a], p.599). We shall return to this system in chapter four.

It is not our intention to consider systems of this nature here. We shall be concerned with systems that aim to represent the law itself and attempt to model and support legal reasoning. What exactly is meant by this, what problems are involved and how the systems we have developed attempt to solve these problems is the main object of the following chapters.

For the time being we shall just make one, important observation. Classical expert systems often give just one, definite answer, when queried. If conflicting approaches exist, the classical systems attach probabilities and certainty factors to their rules. The program then combines these factors to rank its answers and recommendations. A thorough discussion of this approach and its relation to our kind of legal system will be carried out in a later section of this chapter (1.6.3).

One should not expect a legal system to exhibit a behaviour similar to what is usually obtained from expert systems in medicine or science. Consider for example a law-student who is given a hypothetical case as an exercise. He will first have to analyse its facts and spot the important issues of the case. He will then attempt to develop different approaches to each of these issues. Similarly, a lawyer who has been asked to give an opinion on a certain case will examine the facts, noting which aspects of the case have a clear interpretation according to the law, and which aspects of the case are related to points of law which may have several possible interpretations. He will supply arguments both for and against a certain decision according to these various interpretations. One would want a legal computer system to carry out a similar kind of analysis. The system should spot the problematic issues, and for each of them it should find the different approaches and perhaps contradictory conclusions that may be reached. It should of course supply the chain of legal argumentation and reasoning behind its (conflicting) answers and the legal precedents the conclusions are based upon.

To illustrate why a legal advisory system must develop conflicting approaches and often cannot give a single definite answer, we shall consider a concrete example in the next paragraph.

1.5 An Example.

In the Anglo-American Legal System the area of Common-Law Private Nuisance is a subdomain of Torts, which is based entirely on case-law. This law attempts to preserve a balance between two conflicting interests, that of the occupier in using his land as he sees fit, and that of his neighbour in the enjoyment of his land.

There are usually lots of varying circumstances and different factors to be taken into account. Consider for example the following quotation:

"That may be a nuisance in Grosvenor Square which would be none in Smithfield Market, that may be a nuisance at midday which would not be so at midnight, that may be a nuisance which is permanent and continual which would be no nuisance if temporary or occasional only" (Pollock C.B., (1862) Bamford v. Turnley 122 ER 27).

Thus what may be considered a nuisance at one location is not necessarily so at another and certain activities may be quite acceptable at one time of the day while they may not be so at another time. Many other factors (and combinations of factors) may also be of importance. In order to decide whether a certain activity is a nuisance such factors and their combinations must be balanced and weighed against each other. Previous cases may indicate what those factors are to be and how to compare them, but will often not supply a final decision.

Consider the following (hypothetical) case, arising in nuisance:

Mr. White lives in a house with an attached garden. Next door lives Mr. Black whose three children often play football in their garden. It sometimes happens that the football flies over the fence into Mr. White's garden. Once last year the ball even hit Mr. White's house and a window was broken. Mr. Black promptly paid him for the damage.

Mr. White is fed up with this situation. He sues Mr. Black in nuisance, claiming that the children's games spoil his enjoyment of his house and garden. He asks the court for an injunction forbidding the children to play any ball-game in the garden. He claims he is constantly apprehensive about being hit or his property being damaged.

Mr. Black acknowledges the facts as presented by Mr. White, but claims that the ongoing activity does not justify such measures. The ground is not a training-field used by a professional football team, but a private garden used by the owner's children for their innocent games. This playing of games he considers to be a quite reasonable activity. If damage should occur in the future he promises to pay reparations as indeed he has done in the past.

In the above example, several lines of argumentation are possible. On one hand, Mr. White is obviously entitled to the enjoyment of his own premises; on the other hand Mr. Black's children are entitled to play games on their father's property. Mr. White will attempt to show that the games gave rise to a sensible injury, i.e. his lack of ability to use and enjoy his land. On the other hand, previous cases have shown that a defendant is *not* liable in nuisance if he can show that his activity is ordinary and reasonable. So Mr. Black can try to argue that the children's games are indeed ordinary and reasonable. In response, Mr. White may point out that this perhaps is true in some cases, but not if the ball flies onto his property so often and in such a way that his entire family is constantly apprehensive about it. Mr. Black in his turn may then suggest that perhaps Mr. White and his family are too sensitive. For every point brought up by the two sides there will be precedents whose decisions seem to depend mainly on that feature. These decisions are conflicting and should all be taken into consideration by the judge deciding the case at hand.

The kind of advisory system we consider in this book should be able to give computer-support to this kind of legal analysis. It should help the user spot the central issues (sensible damage, ordinary and reasonable use of property etc.). It should retrieve past cases with similar elements and indicate the reasoning leading to the decisions in those cases. We shall see below how one of the systems we have developed, **JURIX,** does this.

1.6 Open Texture.

1.6.1 Introduction.

The notion of open texture is frequently encountered in the relevant legal literature and it is important to our theme. Law and legal concepts are said to exhibit *open texture*: A legal concept has a definition only for cases that have come to court and been decided. For cases which have not yet come to court the exact definition of the legal concept cannot be determined in advance.

Consider for example the concept: "owner of a house". This concept, which may seem to have a well-defined meaning, is often used in our legal example-domain: A house-owner is a competent plaintiff in nuisance. Let us first observe that we are interested in the legal meaning of the concept, which not necessarily coincides with the everyday meaning. Next, we can obviously collect cases where the concept "owner of a house" appears, and extract its particular meaning in each case. This will give us a general idea about the concept, but it cannot supply us with an exact definition of it. When a new case comes to court, there is no way of making an a priori decision whether the plaintiff is indeed a "house-owner" or not. The court may choose to adopt what may be called a 'standard meaning', or a special interpretation used in a previous case (if they are different). However, the court may also decide to give an *entirely* new interpretation of the concept owing to certain new circumstances related to the case, that it wishes to take into account.

The notion of 'open texture' is originally due to Waismann in a paper on Wittgenstein's philosophy [Waismann45] and was introduced in jurisprudence by Hart (see e.g. [Hart61]). In Hart's view open texture is an ineliminable feature of language, to be welcomed rather than deplored. For in this world characterized by a relative unpredictable future, inhabited by creatures confronting diverse and constantly changing circumstances, open texture gives reasonableness and flexibility. When non-standard cases arise they require exercise of judicial discretion. Such discretion, according to Hart, is guided by antecedently specified legal standards which impose legal obligations to exercise that discretion according to those standards. How a computerized system may give advice in such non-standard cases is the major problem to be discussed in this book.

Open texture is most obvious in vague concepts like "reasonable activities" mentioned in the example in the previous section. However, concepts which appear to have a precise meaning do also have open texture. As explained in the case of "house-owner" a court may always decide to adopt a different interpretation than the one so far accepted and used.

In order to emphasize this point, we shall consider yet another example. It is a classical example first given by Hart in [Hart58]. It has attained a canonical status and is used by almost every writer on the subject of open texture:

"A legal rule forbids you to take a vehicle into the public park. Plainly this forbids an automobile, but what about bicycles, roller skates, toy automobiles? What about airplanes? Are these, as we say, to be called "vehicles" for the purpose of the rule or not? If we are to communicate with each other at all, and if, as in the most elementary form of law, we are to express our intentions that a certain type of behaviour be regulated by rules, then the general words we use - like "vehicle" in the case I consider - must have some standard instance in which no doubts are felt about its application. There must be a core of settled meaning, but there will be, as well, a penumbra of debatable cases in which words are neither obviously applicable nor obviously ruled out. These cases will each have some features in common with the standard case; they will lack others or be accompanied by features not present in the standard case.." ([Hart58], p.607).

We can further illustrate the concept of open texture by considering an example from a quasi-legal area first given in [Bench88]. We shall make use of this example below in our discussion of the capabilities of a legal computer system for case-law as it is short and easy to understand. It relates to a fragment of the regulations concerning the award of a heating addition to Supplementary Benefit, one of the Social Security benefits provided in the United Kingdom. The relevant legislation states that a person will receive a heating addition if his place of residence is *hard to heat*. No further definition or description is given of the concept 'hard to heat', and an intentional *vagueness* is thus introduced into the legislation by this open textured concept. The reason for this is an acknowledgement that there is room for discretionary judgment in deciding whether the standard has been met. The meaning is so dependent on individual circumstances, that no legislator could hope to foresee every possibility and make provision for it. In some cases it will immediately be obvious that a certain house is indeed hard to heat while another house obviously will not be hard to heat. However, in many cases the situation is not clear initially.

When an application for a heating addition in such a case is considered by an adjudicating clerk, he *must* make some definite decision for or against the award of the heating addition. Whatever he decides, this decision may then form a precedent for a future case: another adjudicating clerk may decide that the previous decision is relevant to the facts at hand in the new case, or he may distinguish the previous case. Let us call all cases where it is known that the house is hard to heat the 'black area' and all cases where it is known that the house is *not* hard to heat the 'white area'. Each decision in a *real* case will then remove this case from what may be called the 'grey' area, i.e. all cases not yet determined and having no obvious decision. We shall return in a later chapter and discuss the nature of the grey area which will always exist owing to the open texture of legal concepts. Our main interest is how a computerized system may help in narrowing the grey area down.

Closely related to the concept of open texture is the concepts of 'easy' and 'hard' cases. We shall give an oversimplified discussion of these concepts for now. A fuller discussion will appear in chapter two. We shall say that a case is *easy*, if all legal experts agree on its outcome, i.e. it is obvious to which area it belongs, the 'white' or the 'black' one. Otherwise a case will be called *hard.*

Thus, when considering a rule or regulation it is possible to distinguish clear central cases where the rule certainly applies and other cases where there are reasons for both asserting and denying that it applies. In this connection Hart has introduced another commonly used metaphor:

"Nothing can eliminate this duality of a core of certainty and a penumbra of doubt." ([Hart61], p.119).

Thus , if the facts of the case correspond to the core-meaning of a rule the case is 'easy', and the judge must apply the rule. However, if the case is 'hard', i.e. it belongs to the penumbra, the judge is not bound by a specific precedent, and by coming to a decision it may be argued that he 'makes new law'.

Hart's approach to law and open texture is not the only possible one. However, as we shall see in chapter two, other, accepted approaches lead to the same practical conclusions.

We shall conclude this introduction to the concept of 'open texture' by formulating two questions concerning legal advisory systems:

1. When considering a concrete case, how does a computer system know whether it belongs to the 'core of certainty' or to the 'penumbra'?

2. If indeed a particular case belongs to the 'penumbra' what advice should the system give its user?

We shall return below to discuss these questions and their significance for a legal advisory system. At this point it should be clear that owing to the fundamental open texture of law - both statutory and case law - an advisory system may deliver *definite* answers only for 'easy' cases. This should of course be the answer all the experts agree upon, when the issue belongs to what Hart calls 'the core of certainty'. Advisory systems addressing 'hard' cases can only produce an analysis about how the case would be argued one way or another. The issue belongs to 'the penumbra of doubt' and may be argued both ways. Most previous work on legal expert systems has addressed only the part of the problem which relates to 'easy' cases.

1.6.2 Vagueness and Ambiguity.

We have previously observed the fact that law is intrinsically open textured. It has a precise definition only for those individual cases that have come to court and been decided; there is no precise definition for what has still to be tried.

The words "vagueness" and "imprecision" are sometimes used to express the idea of open texture (see e.g. [Negoita85]). We shall *not* consider all those words as synonymous. In the case of the first two, one has in the general non-legal sense, no means of making a decision when required. However, in the case of "open texture" we have exact knowledge in past cases already decided by the courts ("point-wise definition"). As for future decisions we have no knowledge at all. Thus **open-texture** is **vagueness** plus **decision-scheme**. However, the word "ambiguity" has a different meaning altogether, at least for statutory law.

In the case of an ambiguity in statutory law what happens is one of two things: Either the law is reformulated in an unambiguous manner, or the interpretation by an appropriate court will form a precedent to be followed in all future cases. In section 3.2.2.3 we shall discuss the different kinds of vagueness of statutory law.

When we now consider case-law, a formulation of ratio and dicta may of course be ambiguously stated, but there is no difference between ambiguity and open texture in this case; what comes to court will be decided and form a precedent for future cases.

1.6.3 Inapplicable Approaches to Open Texture.

1.6.3.1   Introduction.

There are several possible but inappropriate approaches to open texture. It is of great importance for a proper understanding of an academic system dealing with open texture to realize why some methods are acceptable and some not. We shall consider three such unacceptable methods now and explain why their attempt at representing open texture is not acceptable for the kind of system we are interested in. We shall make use of an example to illustrate the three methods. In an action in nuisance it is a defence for the defendant to claim that his activity was 'reasonable'. The concept 'reasonable activity' expresses the open texture of the law in an obvious way. We shall discuss how one may attempt to represent the concept of a 'reasonable activity' in a computer system.

1.6.3.2 The Method of Approximation.

The method of approximations proposes to replace a vague concept, expressing open texture, by a (supposedly) sharp concept.

As explained above, we shall consider the concept of 'reasonable activity'. Let us also assume that this activity is the creation of noise on the defendant's land. How is it possible to determine whether a noise is 'reasonable' or not?

A builder of a computer system for nuisance may decide to approximate the concept of 'reasonable noise" in the following way. He takes advise from sound-engineers, medical doctors etc. and decides to introduce the following rule: "A noise is reasonable if its loudness is less than 100 decibel". Accordingly, his system would attempt to verify that a defendant is not guilty of nuisance by checking the loudness of the noise against the given threshold.

We shall carry out our discussion in three steps.

1.   Lawyers do not usually apply numerical measurement and quantification to concepts. Yet, one can imagine many applications which are not particularly sensitive to the value decided upon as a threshold where the lawyers would go along with such a working definition.

2. A concept like 'reasonable noise' has several dimensions and cannot be expressed just by its loudness (which is measured in decibels). Besides the loudness of a noise one much consider its pitch, its extent in time and other physically measurable quantities. However, also the location, the time of the day, frequency of occurrence and possibly other factors should be taken into account, when deciding whether a certain noise is 'reasonable' or not. This is precisely the view expressed by Pollock C.B. quoted on p.23.

Still, it may nevertheless be possible to come up with a working approximation of 'reasonable noise'. One would perhaps consult with a more extensive panel of experts, and consider decisions in previous noise-nuisance cases before creating such an approximation.

Of course, a system incorporating such a definition would only be as good or as bad as the definition itself, i.e. depend on the skills of the experts. It would be a system in the style of a classical expert system. In some cases the system would behave very well, while in other cases it would be no good.

3. For the sake of simplicity let us assume that the concept of 'reasonable noise' may be taken as one-dimensional and may be approximated by a single rule like: "The noise is reasonable if its loudness is less than 100 decibel". Let us furthermore assume that this was proposed as a legislative rule. This approach is quite common: Legislative bodies often give legal validity to definitions proposed by panels of experts. But how should the loudness be measured? When? By whom? And under which circumstances? The legislators could never foresee all possible situations of alleged noise-nuisance and provide for them. The conclusion is not surprising: We have exchanged one piece of open textured law by another piece of open textured law, and the supposed sharpness of the newly defined concept is entirely imaginary.

We now return to our computer system. As we have just seen, the new 100-decibel rule has open texture just like the old one. From the point of view of dealing with open texture there is no difference in *principle* if the system asks whether the noise is reasonable or whether the loudness is less than 100 decibels. The difference between the two questions is the following: When asked whether the noise is reasonable, the user may have no idea how to approach the question. When asked about the loudness the user is guided by an expert's interpretation of 'reasonableness'. This is merely a matter of convenience though perhaps a major one. In **both** cases forcing the user to give a definite answer of *yes* or *no* is equivalent to ignoring the open texture (for there may be reasons to answer *both* yes or no to the question).

Our conclusion is therefore that a system which is supposed to represent the law itself cannot apply the approximation method. However, a system which is intended to give correct answers some of the time, but not always, may indeed use this approach.

1.6.3.3 Use of Probability and Fuzzy Logic.

Classical expert systems make prominent use of both probability and fuzzy logic. They sometimes also use so-called certainty factors which have had different interpretations both as concepts of probability and as concepts of fuzzy logic. In showing that both of the two areas ought not to be used in an 'academic' system we shall follow [Bench88] closely.

We shall use the same example, taken from the area of nuisance, as in the previous section. Let us assume that a plaintiff complains that his neighbour is testing a jet-motor in his back-garden but claims that the noise is reasonable. The problem is how to deal with the open texture expressed by the concept 'reasonable noise'.

One approach is to use our common-sense knowledge of jet-motors (which usually are infernally loud) and conclude that the noise emanating from the neighbour's garden *probably* is unreasonable. In a classical type of expert system this is acceptable. In our kind of system it would, however, be no good: We *must* consider the particular motor in the neighbour's garden, and decide whether *its* noise is reasonable or not. Perhaps the neighbour is an inventor trying out his newest invention: A noise-free jet-motor.

Another approach would use a (fictional) statistics saying that 90% of all jet-motors are unreasonably loud. This would help us estimate a priori the probability that a plaintiff would win a nuisance case involving a jet-motor. Still, the statistics would not help us to draw any conclusion for the particular motor in the neighbour's garden. Again we have a method appropriate for an 'experiential' kind of system, but not for an 'academic' one.

Fuzzy logic is described by its originator as a general theory for dealing with vague concepts (see [Zadeh75]). In fuzzy logic the truth-value of a proposition is not limited to just zero or one, but it may also attain any value in between.

Thus "the noise is reasonable" could have the truth-value 1 for a particular electric-shaver motor, the truth-value 0.75 for a particular refrigerator motor, 0.57 for a particular elevator motor and 0 for a particular jet motor. The curve which maps specific instances related to a concept (here: reasonableness of noise) onto the truth-values of the concept is called the truth-profile of the concept.

The question is what interpretation one should give to such truth-values. Proponents of fuzzy logic strongly assert that a probabilistic interpretation is not appropriate. Thus one cannot say that the probability of refrigerator motors in general (or the particular refrigerator motor we are concerned with) being reasonably noisy is 0.75. As fuzzy logic specifically omits to specify how the truth-profiles are to be assigned, we would not know how to choose a truth-value for another kind of motor, or even for another motor of a given type. For another refrigerator motor what would be the significance of choosing the truth-value 0.748 or 0.749? It would presumably mean that this second motor makes more noise than the one mentioned above, but what else is the significance of the numbers?

Fuzzy logic also supplies rules for computing with truth-values: Given the (perhaps fractional) truth-values of individual propositions it is possible to compute the truth-value of any logical expression containing them. There exist different versions of fuzzy logic according to different rules of combining truth-values in logical expressions. It is not clear which versions would be appropriate to deal with open texture and why.

Law seldom provides for degrees of truth: Either a particular noise is reasonable or it is not. Using fuzzy logic one could possibly overcome this problem in the following way. For a given noise one would consider the fuzzy truth-value of the statement: "the noise is reasonable". If this value was over a predetermined threshold (say 0.75) one would decide that the noise is reasonable. If the value was below this threshold, the noise would be considered unreasonable. But this means that the fuzzy logic approach is not really different from the method of approximations discussed in the previous section, where we suggested a threshold for loudness at, say, 100 decibel.

In the case of a more complicated statement one would determine the fuzzy truth-values of its components, compute the fuzzy truth-value of the statement using some set of composition-laws and finally apply the threshold. As pointed out in [Bench88] this lessens the implications of the exact form of the truth-profile. However:

"in most cases it would have the disadvantage of calling the whole approach into question, since the variety of truth values is a central requirement for terms to be given the fuzzy treatment, and one which legal concepts blatantly fail to fulfill" ([Bench88], p.11).

Some attempts have been made to apply fuzzy logic to law. [Thorne80] develops a theory of 'fuzzy negligence' which he asserts is useful for describing the variance of plaintiff's dollar verdicts in negligence actions. [Reisinger82] gives a fuzzy logic algorithm to describe reasoning by analogy in law. It is conceivable that the implementation of such methods would be beneficial in an experiential computer system. However, they do not seem to have a place in an academic type of system.

1.6.3.4   Conclusion.

We have here considered open texture as it is expressed in a concept like 'reasonable noise', and realized why it cannot possibly be approximated by any method. This is an appropriate point to add, that any attempt to eliminate open texture as expressed in a concept like 'vehicle' by substituting an exhaustive list is of course also impossible. We observe again that the idea of open texture is fundamental for the proper functioning of the legal system.

1.7   The Rule-Based and Case-Based Paradigms.

As already mentioned (see p.15) the classical type of expert system is usually a rule-based system, i.e., it uses a knowledge-representation based on rules and applies logical deduction to those rules. This rule-based approach has been used extensively in the legal domain. For example, the experiential system on Latent Damage by Capper and Susskind was actually built using the expert system shell Crystal (see [Susskind89], p.26).

However, as we have previously indicated (in section 1.6.3), using rules - with or without attached probabilities - may not be the only appropriate paradigm for legal systems. Another approach of relevance uses the case-based paradigm.

Case-based reasoning (CBR) involves several operations (see [DARPA89], p.1):

1. Recall from memory of relevant cases to a new, given case.
2. Selection of the most promising case (or cases)
3. Construction of a solution, interpretation or evaluation of the new case.
4. Testing and critique of the output of step 3.
5. Evaluation of results.
6. Updating of memory by storing new case.

The retrieval of cases (step 1) requires that cases are labeled in memory. The Indexing Problem is the problem of how to label (index) these cases and how to retrieve them as needed. Selection of promising cases (step 2) requires that some method of weighing the retrieved cases exists. In the legal domain step 3 is equivalent to utilizing and adapting the retrieved cases (precedents) in order to create lines of argumentation and propose logical rulings for the case at hand. For a general discussion of the Adaption problem, i.e., how to adapt old cases or parts of old cases to a new one see [Kass90]. Overviews of motivations, methods and trends in CBR may be found in [Slade91] and [Kolodner91].

The distinction between statutory-law computer systems and case-law computer systems does not mean that the former must necessarily be rule-based and the latter case-based in the sense just described. For example, Gardner's system (to be described in section 3.4.2) deals with case-law and is rule-based. HYPO (see section 3.4.3.2) deals with case-law and is indeed case-based. CABARET and GREBE (see section 3.4.4) are hybrid systems, i.e., they use both rule-based and case-based reasoning.

In the following chapters we shall attempt to relate those concepts to legal reasoning.

1.8 The Legal Domain of Nuisance.

The following is a brief introduction to the legal domain of nuisance. For reasons to be mentioned later this area of law will form a central example in the book.

Neighbours are people who occupy adjacent pieces of land or adjoining flats in the same buildings. They live in constant physical proximity and they did not choose each other. The common law has a special regime for them and it is called 'nuisance'. This law represents an attempt to preserve a balance between two conflicting interests, that of the occupier in using his land as he thinks fit, and that of his neighbour in the quiet enjoyment of his land. Thus, if, for example, a house-owner's daughter plays the piano every day, and his neighbour is bothered by it, he may sue him in nuisance. However, the neighbour must show that the activity of piano-playing is unreasonable. Ordinary use of musical instruments by neighbours is certainly not unlawful. Only by showing that the playing, e.g. is exceptionally loud, or takes place in the middle of the night etc. can the neighbour win his case. If the house-owner is found liable in nuisance, the court may award damages for past and future sufferings. The court may also grant an injunction, forbidding the playing of the piano in general, or at certain hours etc.

More precisely:

"*Common Law, Private Nuisance* originates in an act or omission whereby a person is annoyed, prejudiced or disturbed in the enjoyment of land, whether by physical damage to the land or by other interference with the enjoyment of the land or with his exercise of an easement, profit or other similar right or with his health, comfort or convenience as occupier of such land." ([Salmond81], p.48).

Legal action may be of two kinds: Criminal proceedings and civil actions. Criminal proceedings are instigated by the appropriate authorities, who accuse the defendant of certain behaviour, which is punishable by a fine paid to the authorities, by confinement in prison or both. Civil action is an action where the plaintiff complains to the court of a wrong committed by the defendant. Among the various kinds of civil action one has an action in contract and an action in tort. Nuisance is one of the torts, and we concentrate specifically on common law (as opposed to statutory), private (as opposed to public) nuisance.

This relatively small and self-contained area of law is based exclusively on case law and will form the central example in our inquiries into the development of legal systems. Without going deeply into the characteristics of this legal subdomain we shall briefly state some common facts:
(1) The tort emphasizes the harm to the plaintiff rather that the conduct of the defendant.
(2) Its main feature is the interest invaded - that of the use and enjoyment of land.

The saying 'sic utere tuo ut alienum non laedas' (use your own property so as not to injure your neighbour) encapsulates the two main features of the nuisance action, namely that liability springs from a condition on the defendant's land and that protection is accorded to the plaintiff's enjoyment of his land. On the other hand, this saying has been much criticized, as it suggests, e.g., that any 'use' of land is actionable if it results in harm to a neighbour's land. That is inaccurate: if a 'use' is *ordinary* and *reasonable*, there is no liability on the defendant for the harm caused to the plaintiff.

Nuisance is a good area to choose for building an advisory system. As we have explained above, this particular area is all about balancing one person's interests against another's, and it is full of concepts like 'ordinary use' and 'reasonable defence', which explicitly express the open texture of the law. Given a particular case in this area, the system we are aiming at should be able to retrieve various arguments and precedents indicating both a certain decision and its converse.

1.9 Example Execution under JURIX (Summary).

To give some impression of **JURIX**, we shall here describe the nature of output one can obtain from **JURIX**, when applying it to a hypothetical example. The legal knowledge of the system is based on the well-known treatise by Salmond on Torts ([Salmond81]). As we shall see, there are undoubtly aspects of this case that relate to negligence, but we shall ignore them. At present **JURIX** has a knowledge-base which relates to nuisance only.

The Facts.

Mr. Smith, a contractor, has been licensed by Mr. Jones, a landowner, to use Mr. Jones' shed, standing on Mr. Jones' farmland, for his ditch-digging tractor. The shed is old, and Mr. Smith has carried out some repairs he felt to be necessary.

Mr. Jones asks Mr. Smith to dig a drainage-ditch on his land right next to the shed. Mr. Smith agrees that the licence to use the shed will be his payment for the digging.

While digging the ditch, Mr. Smith's tractor accidentally hits the shed, and some slates fall off the roof of the shed, onto the neighbouring property owned by Mr. Brown, and damage Mr. Brown's greenhouse.

Mr. Brown sues both Mr. Smith and Mr. Jones for damages in nuisance. Let us consider, for example, the lawyer representing Mr. Jones, the landowner. How should this
lawyer reason about the case, and to what conclusions may he arrive?

Discussion:

Mr. Smith's ditch-digging activity gave rise to the damage, so perhaps he is solely to blame. But then, maybe the party ordering the work can also be found liable.

On the other hand, perhaps the activity of Mr. Smith is not the important feature here, but the state of the shed. It was old and ought to have been repaired. The agreement between Mr. Jones and Mr. Smith did not state who was responsible for repairs. Mr. Smith had in fact been doing such repairs, so perhaps he is responsible for not fixing the loose slates. However, Mr. Jones had access and control over the premises, perhaps he ought to have noticed the disrepair and done something about it?

Furthermore, does it make any difference, whether Mr. Smith pays Mr. Jones for his licence to use the shed by digging the ditch, or was initially allowed to use the shed for free? Is it important if Mr. Jones also uses the shed, for example to store some unused machinery? Would it have made a difference if the tractor had hit the shed during parking maneuvers instead of during work? Finally, perhaps nobody is to blame! Maybe it can be argued that Mr. Brown should not have built his greenhouse in such proximity to the border of Mr. Jones farmland, and if he did, he ought to have responsibility if ordinary and reasonable activities on that land gave rise to damage.

Program Output.

JURIX queries the user in order to establish the facts of the case and help him discover lines of reasoning. For example, when querying the user concerning the liability of the defendant, the knowledge built into the system will lead to enquiries about the status of the defendant: Is he owner-occupier of the premises? Is he a lessee? etc. Among the various possibilities raised by the system two will be relevant to the case at hand.

First line of Reasoning: Defendant is Independent Contractor.

JURIX will quote a general rule: In the absence of carelessness in choosing a competent independent contractor, the employer is not liable for a contractor. If requested to do so, it will cite the cases: Bower v. Peate (1876)1 QBD 321, Matania v. National Provincial Board Ltd. [1936]2 All ER 633 and Spier v. Smee [1946]1 All ER 489, to support the above statement.

Should the user be interested, the system will retrieve sources relating to the concepts of non-delegable duty and strict liability. It should however be clear, that if the landowner, Mr. Jones can show that the contractor, Mr. Smith, is generally considered competent, and that ditch-digging is the relevant nuisance-activity, he will himself probably have no liability in nuisance.

However, the system will also query the user about the length of time of the activity. It will inform him that actions that happen on one occasion only can be considered nuisance if they arise "from the condition of the defendant's land" (quoting Thesiger J. in USCM Ltd. v. W.J.Whittall and Son Ltd. [1970]2 All ER 417, 430). This raises the question about the state of the shed, and who is responsible for its repair.

Second line of Reasoning: Licensor v. Licensee.

When the user wants to retrieve the legal background on this issue, **JURIX** will initially quote an authority as follows: "It will be a rare case where the licensor cannot be held liable for a state of affairs existing on his land. This is because, in nearly-all cases, he retains the right to possession of the land." Thus Mr. Jones, the landlord seems to be liable.

Next, the question is raised about the liability of the licensee. **JURIX** will help the user confirm Mr. Smith's liability, citing 5 cases in order to clarify what control is needed in order for a licensee to be liable. It appears that Mr. Smith may be liable, even if somebody else did the actual harm, or through some other medium than the tractor.

Third line of Reasoning: Nobody is to Blame.

The user may attempt to explore such a line of defence. However, he will be discouraged in this. **JURIX** will point out that (1) the activity must be reasonably undertaken, and (2) the state of affairs must be ordinary. While there seems to be no problems in justifying (1), (2) needs clarification. The system will query the user, among other things, whether the state of affairs was dangerous. As the slates undeniably were loose, this seems to be true, and this line of defence falls through.

Finally, **JURIX** will assist the user in confirming that the present case is hard, and it will summarize the relevant legal information.

As we see, **JURIX** has helped to spot the following issues of the case:

(1) Defendant is Independent Contractor.
(2) Licensor v. Licensee.
(3) No blame of Defendant.

It has supported the reasoning about each of these issues by citing the relevant cases for both sides.

Concerning the third issue: It seems appropriate to say that the user here uses the system to create a hypothetical case. Assume that the tractor never hit the shed, but that the slates fell down all of a sudden. As the state of affairs was dangerous (it is known that the slates were loose), the defendant will be hold liable in this hypothetical case. It therefore seems probable that the same decision would be reached in the case at hand.

The above legal analysis is just the kind that an expert lawyer prepares if asked for an opinion by a client. In practice the opinion is used to determine whether the case should proceed - if so, a legal argument is prepared on basis of the retrieved cases.

1.10 Example Execution under Meta.

1.10.1 Implementation Area.

The implementation area of Meta is related to the advisory activity undertaken in many academic institutions for the benefit of the students. We shall use the regulations and precedents which relate to the registration of undergraduate students for courses in the Department of Mathematics and Computer Science at Bar Ilan University.

There are several reasons for choosing this area. While the kind of problems that arise in the Social Services may be of a more general interest, it seems to be very difficult to find cooperating authorities and officials who agree to make their decisions public. In the academic domain this problem has not arisen. Furthermore, the expertise needed to analyse the domain is available at first hand. Finally, through interviewing the advisors it appeared that they had long felt a genuine need for a computer system to ensure fairness of the decisions and their uniformity over the years. The chosen area is thus far from being a 'toy' area.

The specific problem we have dealt with may be described as follows: Many courses in the department have prerequisites, i.e., other courses which must be passed first. Sometimes a student will apply to an advisor and ask for permission to take a certain course without having passed the prerequisite.

This may be because the student is outstanding in some positive sense and wants to proceed with his studies at a faster rate than usual. Conversely, it may also happen when a student has been unsuccessful in his attempt to pass the prerequisite, but nevertheless wants to register for the given course (and usually also for the prerequisite which thus turns into a corequisite). In the second case the student will usually appeal to some extenuating circumstance in order to justify his application.

Several departmental advisors are engaged in the registration task previous to the beginning of the academic year. While their judgement is not arbitrary it is certainly not uniform. Their activity may be compared to the function of adjudicating clerks described in the introduction. We have observed these advisors during their work and established a case-base on the particular problem of permitting (or denying) registration to undergraduate courses in mathematics, statistics and computer science without fulfillment of the prerequisite requirements.

1.10.2 A Concrete Example (Summary).

The Facts.

A student who has not passed the Data Structures course (called Structures in the following) applies for permission to register for the Theory of Algorithms course (Algorithms for short). His grades so far have been exceptionally good (we shall call him an A-student), and he wants to save time (and money) and begin graduate school ahead of schedule.

Program Output.

Meta retrieves the record of the student from the student master-file. Some further data is obtained by querying the user (student advisor). The system will then proceed to retrieve relevant previous cases, apply them to the one at hand and state the conclusions and the way it has deduced them.

It will first retrieve a case where a student belonging to a special study-scheme (e.g. an Honours-course) was given permission to take Algorithms without having taken Structures. The system will argue that students are selected to that special study-scheme because they are 'good'. As our student is an A-student (and therefore also 'good') he should get the same permission.

However, the system will also point out that the retrieved precedent may be taken as indicating that *only* students belonging to the special scheme may dispense with Structures as a prerequisite. Thus our student should be *denied* permission.

Another concrete case retrieved by Meta relates to an A-student who got permission to take the AI course without having first passed the Advanced Language course (which includes Lisp and Prolog). The system will argue that as the student in the case at hand is an A-student he should also get permission to dispense with his prerequisite - even though different courses are involved.

On the other hand, the system will point out that perhaps the student in the present case should be denied permission despite the fact that he is an A-student. It is possible that the precedent relates only to the AI and Advanced Languages courses but not to Algorithms and Structures.

The above analysis is the one a human advisor would carry out, assuming he could remember the previous relevant cases. The system weights the arguments (as we shall explain in section 6.3), but leaves the final decision to the human user.

1.11 Overview of Further Contents.

In the previous sections we have indicated the aims of this book: To deal with computer systems in areas that depend on human discretionary judgment, specifically in the area of case-law. We can describe these aims in a more precise manner:

1. To discuss problems that relate to open texture and to common-sense knowledge, and to examine the possibility of building computer systems for case-law using either a rule-based or a case-based paradigm. We shall examine existing systems and show that they cannot provide much *practical* advice at their present, prototypical stage of development. Following our analysis of previous work it will appear that the problems of giving practical advice on case-law are extremely difficult.

2. To describe the building of a legal computer system, **JURIX**, based on secondary sources to advise and support a human user in analyzing a given case. The system uses rules derived from an authoritative treatise in a way which is different from the way previous researchers have used such rules. We do not follow the rule-based approach and apply the rules in a deductive manner, but build a system which helps the user carry out a rule-guided analysis of his problem. in other words, the rules are used as indices in a case-based system.

3. To describe the building of a computer system, Meta, intended for quasi-legal domains. The system uses manually extracted rules as indices to a case-base. It creates additional (and sometimes conflicting) rules by applying meta-rules. By using the new and old rules selectively the system can simulate legal reasoning in the specified quasi-legal domain and thus support its user.

The following chapters will present and support these aims in the following manner: The first step must be to discover *exactly* what problems arise when one attempts to build a legal computer system. Some of those problems have already been indicated and will be discussed in full in the following chapters.

Some of the problems must certainly be related to the fact that our domain of application is law and not, say, medicine. It seems therefore natural to begin an inquiry by considering some fundamental issues in jurisprudence. This shall be carried out in the next chapter, and we shall mainly base our discussion on [Susskind87]. This will end the first, introductory part of the book.

The second part deals with the work carried out by other researchers in the field, both in the area of statutory law and in the area of case law. Chapter three describes the projects themselves, the problems they ran into and the attempts at solving these problems. In Chapter four we critically consider the related work and some of our own ideas in light of the jurisprudential preliminaries. Our conclusion is that actual reasoning with case-law, weighing conflicting arguments and decisions is an extremely difficult problem. Previous projects have only begun to approach this goal.

Part three is devoted to a description and discussion of our systems. Chapter five will discuss the motivation for developing **JURIX** in view of the previous work. We shall attempt to justify the approach we have used, explain the theoretical background of the system and evaluate it in comparison to the other systems. A short description is also given of the system itself. Chapter six will describe Meta, its design and operation.

Finally, chapter seven summarizes the work. It considers the goals we have set ourselves, and the extent to which they can and have been fulfilled. We also discuss various approaches that may be worthwhile to take in future research and the problems hereby involved.

2

Jurisprudential Preliminaries

> The law is a sort of hocus-pocus science,
> that smiles in yer face while it picks
> yer pocket; and the glorious uncertainty
> of it is of mair use to the professor than
> the justice of it.
> (Charles Macklin, Love a la Mode, 1759)

2.1 Introduction.

In chapter one we gave a short overview of the Anglo-American legal system and devoted some space to define and discuss the concept of open texture. For a jurist that may have been superfluous, but for a computer scientist interested in legal computer systems much more background on law and legal concepts is actually needed.

No instant course in law or jurisprudence is possible. Even a comprehensive study of the important legal issues cannot be undertaken within this framework. What follows should therefore be considered as a presentation of some legal concepts which are central to our topic of legal systems and a short survey of some related jurisprudential approaches.

Richard Susskind has written a massive work, [Susskind87], about legal computer systems addressed to jurisprudential scholars. Its significance may possibly be lost on computer scientists, so we shall attempt to present the main points of Susskind's comprehensive work in terms that computer scientists would understand.

Susskind has several aims in his work:

(1) To consider what is a legal expert system.

(2) To determine what can and what cannot be left to a legal expert system according to jurisprudence.

(3) To determine the limits of consensus among the theorists of jurisprudence.

(4) To propose models for legal expert systems based on those domains of agreement.

He deals mainly with statutory law, but much of his work also relates to our domain of case-law systems.

Computer scientists are accustomed to examine problems in the expert system area from three aspects:

(1) Knowledge acquisition.
(2) Knowledge representation.
(3) Knowledge utilization.

Each of these aspects may of course be considered from a computer science viewpoint. We shall indeed do exactly that in chapter four. However, they can also be viewed from the side of jurisprudence. Especially the latter two topics are jurisprudentially interesting. In considering these issues we shall follow [Susskind87] very closely, though we are making no attempt at completeness, and the discussion is structured differently.

2.2 Knowledge Acquisition.

2.2.1 Introduction.

Before considering problems of knowledge acquisition, representation and utilization we must make it clear what kind of legal knowledge we are talking about.

In the introduction we already distinguished between two kind of legal expert systems: One kind based on a representation of the law and reasoning with the law, and the other kind based on experience of legal practitioners. Following Susskind we have called the former an 'academic' system and the latter an 'experiential' system. It would seem that the two kinds of systems would need different knowledge sources, and hence different methods of acquisition.

In order to specify what the knowledge-sources should be, and in order to work with some exact terminology, it is convenient to introduce a series of definitions (from [Susskind87]) stated in an informal manner.

2.2.2 Definitions.

(1) We begin with a concept which will enable us to name the original source-material of an academic system:

Law-formulations are those widely accepted sources of legal systems: Legislation and Case-Reports.

(2) It may sometimes be of importance to keep the exact law-formulations in the computer for documentary purposes. However, they are not suited for any kind of other activity that we have in mind. There is therefore a need for two additional concepts:

Statute law-statements are statements about what the content of the statutory law is.

The law-statements should be equivalent to the law-formulations in content and generality. They may well be expressed in identical terms to the law-formulations that they describe.

In the next chapter we shall describe two computer systems for statutory law. They will naturally use a computer formalization of the law-statements. We shall see below in (4) other possibilities exist.

As we have already mentioned, the judge does not state the ratio decidendi in an explicit manner, and a law-report may contain much material which is not of equal significance. As Susskind remarks:

"Many judgments embrace a complex web of legal history, expressions of moral (personal or popular), social, political, sexual and religious preferences, portions of descriptive, interpretative, predictive or derivative legal science, as well, of course, as descriptions of the facts of the instant case and the relevant legal arguments. From such arrays of legal, quasi-legal and non-legal data, judges, lawyers, legal scientists, legal officials, legal theorists, and citizens have to pluck their interpretations of the rules of law considered to be embedded in the reports." ([Susskind87], p.63).

The jurisprudential literature on the subject of whether and how to determine the ratio decidendi is very extensive, and it appears without consensus. Nevertheless, Susskind brings evidence to support the view that it can practically always be done. We shall here restrict ourselves to a quotation from [Hart61] on this subject, which is also cited by Susskind:

"Any honest description of the use of precedent in English law must allow for the following pairs of contrasting facts. First, there is no single method of determining the rule for which a given authoritative precedent is an authority. Notwithstanding this, in the vast majority of decided cases there is very little doubt. The head-note is usually correct enough. Secondly, there is no authoritative or uniquely correct formulation of any rule to be extracted from cases. On the other hand, there is often very general agreement, when the bearing of a precedent on a later case is in issue, that a given formulation is adequate." ([Hart61], p. 131)

There is therefore good reason for introducing the following concept:

Case law-statements are (provisional) interpretations of case-law considered similar to statute law-statements.

A definition like the above raises a central question for jurisprudence and therefore also for legal systems: If we are able to formulate statutory law-statements and case law-statements for all precedents, does this mean that the entire statutory and common-law system may be reduced to a collection of such statements, or, as we shall call them in the future: 'rules'? If the answer is affirmative, how can we process these rules? If there is more to law than rules, what is that? and how do we confront it in a computer system? These are major issues in jurisprudence which we shall return to below.

The fact that both statutory law and case-law may be represented (at least partially) by rules raises another interesting and relevant question. Can legal computer systems for statutory law and case-law have the same form, i.e., be constructed with the same type of knowledge base? This question is of course intimately connected to the first and will also be considered below.

(3) The two forms of law-statements defined above will obviously form the basis of a knowledge-base for an academic system. The two concepts which we shall define below are of central importance for the alternative kind of legal system mentioned before (the experiential system). They may be called legal heuristics.

Statute law-predictions are predictions of the probability of a statute law-statement being adopted or applied by the courts.

In order to present examples for this and other definitions we need some topic from statutory law. Our examples from the introduction were taken from the common-law area of nuisance and are therefore not applicable here.

In section 3.2.3 we shall consider a system for (statutory) income tax law. Among other things the program recognizes what is called a B-reorganization of a corporation. This simply means that the corporation buys the stock of another corporation for all its own stock and distributes it among its stock-holders. The U.S. Income Tax Law holds that the stock-holders in such a B-reorganization are *exempt from taxation* of the new stock they have received.. A statute law-prediction could then be:

"If it is a B-reorganization, there is a probability of 0.99 that the courts will grant a tax-exemption."

In other words, this law-prediction tells us what the probability is that the court will apply the statute law-statement concerning tax-exemption in the case of a B-reorganization (and not, say, some other rule).

Case law-predictions are made in two circumstances:

(i) When it is impossible to formulate a ratio decidendi, a case law-prediction is made of the court's likely interpretation.

(ii) When a provisional case law-statement can be made, it may be desirable to supplement the rendition of the indisputable ratio with a probabilistic case law-prediction.

Neither kind of law-prediction has a place in an academic system. The law-predictions could, however, be used in an experiential one. They may be developed by the use of methods of jurimetrics, which we shall consider in section 3.3. Similar rules could also be elicited from a human expert who may have developed informal rules of his own based on his experience in court.

(**4**) Susskind remarks that a computer system which stores only representations of law-statements may be practically useless, as the law-statements are invariably cast in very general terms. For example, a system which only could query the user: "Is it a B-reorganization?" would not be very useful. On the other hand, a system, which had knowledge about several particular situations which could be considered B-reorganizations, would be of greater use. It is therefore desirable to enable less abstract and more particular concepts to be represented in the knowledge-base. To that end he suggests supplementing the system-knowledge of law-statements with knowledge of law-derivations:

Statute law-derivations are obtained by substituting special cases in statute law-statements.

As an additional example of this kind, consider a system using some law-statement containing the concept of 'vehicle' which we considered at some length in section 1.6.1. A statute law-derivation may then substitute 'motorcycle' for 'vehicle'.

Case law-derivations are similarly derived from the case law-statements.

In connection with the concept of law-derivations Susskind mentions two possible approaches to legal reasoning:

(i) Classification of the facts of the case at hand in general terms and then subsumption of that classification within the terms of one or more legal rules. This may be termed a *'bottom up'* approach.

(ii) Rules are broken down into derivations which are then applied. This may be called a *'top down'* approach.

An interesting question suggests itself following this classification. What is the approach used by existing legal computer systems which attempt to deal with legal reasoning. Do they execute according to a 'bottom up' approach or according to a 'top down' one? Which method is appropriate and under what circumstances? We shall return to this question in chapter four, after having surveyed various systems.

(**5**) We have already mentioned the possibility that the scope of a ratio decidendi will be narrowed or widened with time. The legal scientist may guess how the ratio might be developed. In order to operate with that possibility it is convenient to define:

Case law-generalizations which are extensions or generalizations of the ratio.

Susskind remarks, that it is unlikely that the generalization of statutory law statements would be of interest. It is generally assumed that the terms of a statute constitute the upper limit of generality, which a court would not want to extend.

2.2.3 Methods of Acquisition.

In the previous section we determined some of the sources of the legal knowledge-base of a computer system. The question arises how to acquire this knowledge.

Many topics addressed by Susskind relate to the role of a so called 'knowledge engineer'. Such a person has a well-determined role in the creation of an expert system of the classical type. He is responsible for the elicitation of knowledge from the expert. In an experiential system such a person definitely has a role, as has been documented over and over again (see [Wellbank83]).

In the experiential system the knowledge engineer would be responsible for extracting, what may be called *heuristics*, from the expert. This knowledge is related primarily to law-derivations, law-generalizations and law-predictions (and of course the expert's own empirical knowledge). A problem which may arise is of course that a human expert may set a very high price before agreeing to participate in a knowledge elicitation process.

The construction of such systems is well understood among builders of expert systems, and the development of an experiential system is therefore mainly a commercial proposition. Several such systems have indeed been built (see, e.g. [Susskind87], p.200 for a tabular survey of some legal systems - academic and experiential). The system by Capper and Susskind himself relating to the Latent Damage Act 1986 is described in section 1.4. In chapter three we shall examine several approaches to legal systems which will have applicability for experiential systems.

In an academic system, however, the knowledge sources consist primarily and perhaps exclusively of law-statements, which are readily accessible. They may be extracted from formal publications and authoritative treatises. They would have to be interpreted by a person with legal knowledge and expertise, but the particular role of a knowledge engineer could perhaps be eliminated or rather taken over by the system builder himself.

We shall return several times in the following to the (apparent) difference between the two kinds of systems.

2.3 Knowledge Representation.

2.3.1 Introduction.

In this section we shall consider the problem of knowledge representation from a jurisprudential view. In the previous section we examined the various legal knowledge sources and gave some basic definitions in order to name the various concepts. We have already remarked, that from these definitions one can perhaps get the impression that all there is to law can be expressed by rules derived from the various legal sources. A computer-representation of legal knowledge could then also apply rules.

This would bring the creation of an academic computer system within the logic-programming paradigm. The law could be formalized as Prolog-rules and queries could be answered by using the built-in inference engine.

It appears however that different jurisprudential schools have considered rules in different ways. We shall now briefly discuss these approaches. We shall first consider the extreme views: (1) Nothing is rules, and: (2) Everything in legal reasoning is rules. Afterwards we shall discuss two intermediate views, which in the present time seem to hold broad consensus, i.e. that rules are central in any legal reasoning but are not the exclusive medium for representing law. We shall see what the position of rules is in the jurisprudential views of Hart and Dworkin, how to represent the rules and derive appropriate computer representations from them.

2.3.2 Rule Skeptics.

The jurisprudential school of American Legal Realism may be characterized as holding the opinion that judges do not come to their decisions solely on the basis of law-statements. In other words, legal reasoning is not necessarily rule-governed, and logical deduction is not always applicable.

For Jerome Frank, one of the extreme advocates of this approach, legal rules had primarily the function of *ex post facto rationalization* of decisions ([Frank49], p.140). This means that judges may start with a conclusion and then select premises which will justify or rationalise it. A typical quotation by another proponent of the school is:

"rules are important so far as they help you predict what the judges will do" ([Llewellyn51], p.9).

Another formulation of the rule skepticism is the dispute theory of law. As the same proponent of approach puts it:

"What the officials do about disputes is, to my mind, the law itself." ([Llewellyn51], p.12).

If the rule skeptics were right about legal reasoning, then there would no place at all for academic computer systems. On the other hand, experiential systems could very well be developed. They would be based on quite different rules describing the practices of the courts in general, specific knowledge about specific judges etc.

Rule skeptics have been widely criticised for their views. However, the general view held today agrees that in *difficult questions* lawyers must look beyond law-statements and seek to predict court decisions. These 'difficult questions' are what we have called 'hard' cases in the introduction. In 2.4 we shall give a more detailed account of this concept.

2.3.3 Analytic Jurisprudence.

While some of the rule skeptics may have gone to one extremity and entirely denied the use of rules, some of the proponents of analytic jurisprudence went to the other extreme. They looked for a scheme whereby they could exhibit the entire body of law as a system of logical values. Their aim was to understand a legal system as a logically self-consistent whole.

The work of Wesley Hohfeld may be considered within this framework. His work was directed towards concrete problems although he believed that it might render the entire system coherent.

In two papers: [Hohfeld13] and [Hohfeld17] he proposed a system of basic concepts in a scheme of 'opposites' and 'correlatives':

Opposites:	right	privilege	power	immunity
	no-right	duty	disability	liability
Correlatives:	right	privilege	power	immunity
	duty	no-right	liability	disability

These concepts are considered as relations among individuals and their actions. For example: If it is the *right* of X that his neighbour Y shall not create a nuisance, then it is the *duty* of Y not to create such nuisance. If it is X's *privilege* to create such nuisance for himself on his own land, then it is Y's *no-right* that X shall *not* do so.

The purpose of his theory is to discuss the methods by which such concepts are actually applied in judicial reasoning. Hohfeld considers the defined concepts to be what he calls "the lowest common denominators in law" ([Hohfeld13], p.58). This may enable us:

"not only to discover essential similarities and illuminating analogies in the midst of what appears superficially to be infinite and hopeless variety, but also to discern common principles of justice and policy underlying the various jural problems involved." ([Hohfeld13], p.59).

While the general view held today agrees that rules and logical deduction occupy a central position in legal reasoning, extreme approaches are not accepted. As we mentioned above, in difficult questions (and we shall have to define this concept precisely) the rules representing law-statements do not suffice for finding an answer.

2.3.4 Contemporary Views.

In the introduction we already defined the concept of open texture and mentioned some views of H.L.A. Hart on the subject (see section 1.6.1). We shall now expand upon these views and consider them within the present framework.

It appears that Hart basically accepts a rule-based approach. When the meaning of the words of a rule makes it applicable to a given facts situation, he agrees to apply logical deduction. But each rule has a 'penumbra of doubt', where it is not known whether the rule applies or not. If a case belongs to the 'core of certainty' we are allowed to apply the rule. But in cases which relate to the penumbra it is not possible to rely on deductive logical inference. Hart believes the judge can then decide the case at his own discretion.

As Hart says:

"Where the rules are vague, all we can do is to predict what the judges will say" ([Hart83], p.168).

and:

"when the area of open texture is reached very often all we can profitably offer in answer to the question: "What is the law of the matter?" is a guarded prediction of what the courts will do." ([Hart61], p.143).

When considering penumbral cases Susskind suggests to apply law-derivations which may reduce the vagueness of the original law-statement. As we shall see in chapter five, this is essentially the approach of our system, **JURIX**.

A different view is held by Dworkin:

"It is a very popular idea among lawyers that the vagueness of the language they use guarantees that inevitably there will be no right answer to certain legal questions. But the popularity of this idea is based on a failure to discriminate between the fact and the consequences of vagueness in canonical legal language." ([Dworkin85], p.128).

He argues that a proper legal base consists not only of rules but also what he denotes principles and policies:

"The difference between legal principles and legal rules is a logical distinction. Both sets point to particular decisions about legal obligation in particular circumstances, but they differ in the character of the direction they give. Rules are applicable in an all-or-nothing fashion. If the facts a rule stipulates are given, then either the rule is valid, in which case the answer it supplies must be accepted, or it is not, in which case it contributes nothing to the decision." ([Dworkin67], p.25).

Principles, however, must be weighed and balanced:

"When principles intersect....one who must resolve the conflict has to take into account the relative weight of each. This cannot be, of course, an exact measurement, and the judgment that a particular principle or policy is more important than another will often be a controversial one. Nevertheless, it is an integral part of the concept of a principle that it has this dimension, that it makes sense to ask how important or how weighty it is" ([Dworkin67], p.27).

Dworkin believes that every case has a right answer and that it is the job of the judge to find this answer. Judges may make mistakes, but that does of course not mean that they should not make an effort to produce just decisions.

This controversy between Hart and Dworkin has little importance in practice, i.e. for the builder of computer systems. According to Hart the right decision does not exist previously, but is created ('legislated') by the judge. According to Dworkin the right decision exists, but is unknown. From a practical point of view this makes no difference.

2.3.5   Conclusion.

We see that an appropriate knowledge representation in the legal domain may be given by rules. However, these rules are not always of validity. This problem of validity will be considered in the next section.

2.4 Easy vs. Hard Cases.

In the previous section we dealt with a concept we called 'a difficult case'. Actually, we already used this concept in the introduction when we distinguished between 'easy' and 'hard' cases. We shall now give a more precise definition of these concepts.

Susskind first makes the very important observation that there is no such thing as a 'clear' rule. One may speak about a 'clear' or 'easy' case, i.e. a case where it is *clear* that a certain rule may indeed be applied. A case is 'hard' if not 'easy'.

There is also a need to distinguish between *potentially easy* and *retrospectively easy* cases. When a legal expert is confronted with a case and states the opinion that it is 'easy' it may mean two things:

(1) He may consider a decision already delivered by a court which has confirmed his own conclusions of the case.

(2) He may consider a case which has not yet come to court. In that case he states that should the case come to court the decision would undoubtly confirm his opinion.

Such an 'easy' case would usually not be litigated. For counsel for the two sides would agree to the potential outcome of the case in court and settle the matter between their clients. If nevertheless such a case does come to court, the reason is usually that the two opposing sides do not agree about the *facts* of the case. The court is therefore called upon to determine what exactly the facts are and deliver its decision accordingly.

It is still not obvious what exactly makes a case easy. Hart first formulated what Susskind calls a *semantic* approach to 'easy' cases which may be expressed as follows:

"A case is clear where our *common linguistic usage* of the terms of law and ordinary language allow us - beyond all sensible doubt and independent of any alleged purpose of the law-statements in question - to subsume the facts of the case within the terms of the acontextual meaning of the relevant law-statement(s), as conveyed by the verbal law-formulation." ([Susskind87], p.187).

We shall call this the semantic definition. Fuller and the later Hart considered the above formulation insufficient. The later view is stated as follows in what will be called the purposive definition:

"...clear cases in law 'are those in which there is general agreement that they fall within the scope of a rule' and this agreement, he [Hart] says, is both rooted in the 'shared conventions' of the legal and ordinary use of words and connected to *'the purpose'* of statutory provisions." ([Susskind87], p.153).

In other words, a case, easy on the semantic model, would not be easy on the purposive model, if the *purpose* of the legal rules in question seemed to indicate a different conclusion.

We shall give a concrete example of this. We first recall the example given in the introduction concerning the open texture related to the concept of 'vehicle' in connection with a rule forbidding the entrance of vehicles to a park. [Fuller58] considers the case of World-War II veterans driving an old but fully functional army-truck into the park in order to put it on a pedestal. Will this case come under the rule forbidding entrance to the park?

According to the 'semantic' definition the case is 'easy'. If entrance was gained the veterans are guilty. For the army-truck is clearly a 'vehicle' in the semantic sense. However, according to the 'purposive' definition they would be entitled to drive the truck into the park, for their purpose (of putting the truck on a pedestal) would not oppose the purpose of the rule (to prevent 'vehicles' driving around in the park).

2.5 Knowledge Utilization.

From our previous discussions in this chapter it should by now be clear that contemporary legal experts are of the opinion that it is jurisprudentially acceptable to build a legal expert system using a rule-based knowledge representation and logical deduction for 'easy' cases.

This raises the question of the purpose of such a system. We have already mentioned that 'easy' cases are seldom litigated. The major use of such a system would therefore be for a lawyer giving advice to a client about the legal situation related to given facts.

One could perhaps also imagine a layman using such a system. The objection to this would be that a layman may not know whether a case was 'easy' or 'hard'. He may mistakenly apply such a computer system on a 'hard' case and reach entirely wrong conclusions. This would be a simple trap to fall into, especially in a system using a 'bottom up' approach. The user would be called upon to give the facts of the case. But only a person with the appropriate legal background could know what the relevant facts are and how they should be interpreted in order to decide whether a case was 'easy' or 'hard.' We shall return to this issue in chapter four.

This brings us to some other objections related to the use of logical deduction. Some theorists consider the process of *adopting* and *formulating* the premises of a case as a non-deductive issue. We raised the problem of determining what the facts are already in the introduction. An initial human judgment is needed in classifying and *subsuming* the facts of a case within the terms of the knowledge-base.

However, the human user may seek assistance from legal heuristics, so that at least part of the process can be carried out deductively by an expert system, though an experiential one. For the academic system the fundamental assumption seems to be that the facts of the case are well-known and undisputable.

If indeed it is possible to build legal computer systems for 'easy' cases, we are still left with the 'hard' cases. In the introduction we raised two questions concerning such cases: How should a computer system distinguish 'hard' from 'easy' cases and what should it do in 'hard' cases. We have not found any clear answer to either question in this chapter. If it is known that the case is 'hard' one could apply 'experiential' methods to it, and obtain probabilistic answers foreseeing the outcome of the case. However, in an academic system there is no answer in a 'hard' case. The system should be able to retrieve the reasons why the case is 'hard', i.e. argumentations for why a certain rule both may and may not be applied to the case. But no single definite answer is possible in this case.

We have a final remark concerning 'easy' vs. 'hard' cases. The issue of distinguishing between them seems very fundamental in the rule-based paradigm. However, using a case-based paradigm it may actually not be so important. One possibility is to build a system which given the facts of a case will retrieve the relevant cases (for and against a certain decision) and leave it at that. The human user could then decide whether the case at hand is 'easy' or 'hard' and use the output of the system to draw his conclusions accordingly.

2.6   Conclusion.

In this chapter we have attempted to give a minimal introduction to relevant legal concepts for computer scientists. We have discussed what sources of law are at the disposition of an expert systems builder and differentiated between the sources for an experiential and an academic system. We have especially examined the possibility of using a rule-based approach to the knowledge representation, and logical deduction as an inference engine. We have seen that this approach is acceptable for 'easy' cases, but not for 'hard' ones. On the other hand, a case-based approach seems feasible without any need to distinguish between these concepts.

In the next part of the book we shall see what workers in the field have actually accomplished. We shall discover that some of them do not mention the 'easy'/'hard' issue explicitly, or determine what use of their system may be considered jurisprudentially sound. We shall therefore have to interpret their work on our own. The final part of the book will consider the approaches chosen in building **JURIX** and Meta, in view of the present jurisprudential material and systems created by other workers.

PART TWO

Related Work: Factual Description and Critique

3

Related Work

Let us consider the Reason of the Case,
for nothing in Law that is not Reason.
(Sir John Powell, Coggs v. Bernard, 1703)

3.1 Preliminaries.

In the first part of this book we stated that the aim of our work was to deal with computer systems in the legal area. We indicated some of the problems that arise in this area and also discussed some of the jurisprudential aspects of such work.

Time has now come to examine work carried out in the past by researchers in this field and related fields. There are several reasons for considering their work.

1. As a matter of principle one ought to review all background material for the sake of completeness.

2. One of our objects is to estimate the degree of difficulty and the problems that arise when attempting to build legal systems. One way to do that is of course to observe the problems that have arisen in past work and the way researchers have gone about trying to solve them.

3. It seems quite natural that future systems build upon previous work. One may possibly adapt some of the methods and ideas from previous works and apply them in future systems.

We shall divide the chapter into four parts. The first part will deal with work related to statutory law. Even if this work is not directly related to our object, we may still gain some insight that can be of help when considering case-law systems and open texture. The second part is concerned with jurimetrics. We shall consider work which pertains to our problem of building a computer system for case-law, but relates more to an experiential kind of system than to an academic one. In this part of the chapter we shall also discuss work done in the field of information retrieval concerning the retrieval of cases from a given database according to various criteria. Some of this relates to experiential systems, some to academic ones. The third part will deal with some existing computer systems for case law. This part is obviously of greatest importance for our inquiry. The fourth and final part of this chapter shall describe some methods which perhaps not are directly applicable to the kind of computer systems we are aiming at, but nevertheless are of great importance to our work. We shall deal with two proposed approaches to open texture. One of these aims at developing a computational theory of open texture, while the other proposes to capture the nature of open texture through rule generation in a specific way to be described. The second of these methods forms the basis for the the approach used in the Meta system.

The following chapter (chapter four) will classify legal computer systems. It will discuss, compare and summarize the work reported in this chapter according to the classifications to be established. An attempt will also be made to draw conclusions for future work.

3.2 Statutory Law Systems.

3.2.1 Introduction.

Many computer systems have been developed based on statutory law in several areas of law. Such systems are interesting insofar that they deal with legal analysis. Among these systems we shall choose two for a close consideration. One of them, which deals with the British Nationality Act (1981) is of special interest as it uses methods of Logic Programming. It does not deal with open texture as such. However, as law is always open textured, certain assumptions concerning open texture must have been made. The other system (TAXMAN I) deals with American income tax law. It is of interest for us mainly because it precedes the TAXMAN II project which addresses problems of open texture.

3.2.2 Formalization of Statutory Law.

3.2.2.1   Introduction.

The formalization of the British Nationality Act 1981 (BNA) was undertaken as an experiment to test the suitability of Prolog logic for expressing and analyzing legislation mechanically (see [Sergot86] and [Sergot86a]). The BNA was introduced to provide a new definition of British citizenship. It is relatively self-contained, and at the time of the original implementation (1983) the Act was free of the influence of case-law.

From our point of view there are two important issues to consider in relation to this system:

(1) Representation and Reasoning with Statutory Law.
(2) The use of Logic Programming methods.

3.2.2.2 Representation and Reasoning with Statutory Law.

The implementation consists of expressing the Act in Prolog clauses. As a computer system it can then be used for answering queries concerning the citizenship status of an individual. In order to do so the system must have access to facts relating to the particular individual.

These items of information can be supplied in different ways, an issue we shall consider in the next chapter. In this project it is done dynamically by running the program under APES ([Hammond83], [Hammond84]). This system was initially developed as an expert system shell, and is itself implemented in Prolog. It will automatically generate the appropriate queries to the user ([Sergot83]).

For example the first clause of the Act deals with the acquisition of British Citizenship at birth:

"1.-(1) A person born in the United Kingdom after commencement shall be a British Citizen if at the time of birth his father or mother is
　　　(a) a British citizen; or
　　　(b) settled in the United Kingdom."

The Act states that "after commencement' means after or on the date on which the Act

comes into force. As our intention is only to illustrate the program, we shall make some
tacit, simplifying assumptions about the Act and its encoding.

The above clause of the act can then be represented by the following rules, which may
be considered as statutory law-statements in a Prolog-like form:

```
x is-a-british-citizen-on-date y     if   x was-born-in-the-UK
                                     and  x was-born-on-date y
                                     and  y is-after-or-on-commencement
                                     and  z is-a-parent-of x
                                     and  z qualifies-under-1.1-on-date y

z qualifies-under-1.1-on-date y      if   z is-settled-in-UK-on-date y
                                     or   z is-a-british-citizen-on-date y
```

Let us now assume that the system is queried under APES whether an individual, say
Peter, is a British citizen on a given date. Dialogue is then generated where the computer
asks questions like:

"Is it true that Peter was born in the U.K.?"

After completion of the step where the user is queried, the kind of conclusions the system
may reach can have the form:

"Yes, I confirm that Peter is a British citizen on date ..."

The APES system has a built-in explanatory facility, which may be applied during the
computation or when a final conclusion is reached. It constructs proofs of its conclusions, if
requested to do so. If, for example, asked to explain how it proved that Peter is a British
citizen on a specific date, it will give an answer of the form:

"I deduced Peter is a British citizen on date ... from the rule:
x is-a-british-citizen-on-date y **if** x was-born-in-the-UK **and** ...
I can show
1. Peter was born in the UK
2. ....
etc."

The execution of a logic programming representation of the law together with the APES-explanations may thus interpreted as a *legal analysis* of the law with respect to the facts supplied by the query-the-user mechanism.

The main issue that interests us is the problem of dealing with open texture. It appears that there are three distinct ways of looking at this topic with respect to the given system.

1. One may argue that the formalization of the BNA in Prolog clauses yields a single, fixed interpretation of the law and thus totally ignores the open texture of the law.

Consider, for example, the concept "was born in the U.K.". If we assume (with Hart) that law is intrinsically open textured, this is of course also true for any law relating to "was born in the U.K.". However, the open texture is lost the moment we create a Prolog clause making use of the definite predicate: "x was-born-in-the-UK".

2. The above viewpoint may, however, be slightly varied. We may argue that the representation of the law (i.e. the Prolog clauses and their predicates) expresses the open texture no less than the law-formulation itself (i.e. the official Act).

If this is so, then it will be incorrect to state that open texture is actually ignored by the formalization. Rather, there is a lack of *consideration* of open texture. This arises from the use of the query-the-user faculty of APES for input of data, where the user is forced to give clear yes/no answers.

This rigidity is equivalent to ignoring the open texture of the law. For the answer to a question like: "Is it true that Peter was born in the U.K.?" must be a definite yes or no, while for cases in the 'penumbra' the answer could be *both* yes and no.

3. There is a third way of looking at this issue, as follows: The formalization preserves the open texture of the law (as in **2.**), but the system is applicable only for cases where the answer to the queries of the system indeed is precisely yes or no.

This means that the system is applicable only in 'easy' cases, which is in accordance with Susskind's ideas described in the previous chapter. For in an 'easy' case the answer to the question: "Is it true that Peter was born in the U.K.?" is indeed yes or no.

3.2.2.3 The Use of Logic Programming methods.

The representation of statutory law as a computer program has been carried out in several other projects (see [Sergot91] for a survey of these projects and their references). They may in general be divided into two classes. In one class of projects the statutes are represented implicitly in the program, which is usually written in a procedural language. In the other class of programs the law has an explicit representation, separate from the program-part that apply to it. The BNA-program of course belongs to latter class.

It is worthwhile emphasizing that a system may use Prolog, but still belong to the former class. Consider, for example, a computer system for income-tax computation. Such a program is often written in the procedural language COBOL. The program will be based upon the relevant legislation. However, there will be no specific rule, command (or file) where this legislation is concentrated. Rather, the procedural implications of the legislation are translated into COBOL and merged together with other necessary COBOL commands in an inseparable manner. Now this very program may also be written in Prolog, using the same algorithmic approach, "translated", as it were, from COBOL to Prolog. If the programming is carried out correctly, the Prolog program will of course yield the correct result. However, if the execution strategy of the Prolog-interpreter were to be changed, the program would *not* behave correctly.

An example of this kind of Prolog system is Schlobohm's program ([Schlobohm85]) in the area of U.S. Income Tax (section 318(a)). According to [Sergot91] it is nevertheless fairly easy to identify those parts of the program which express legal rules.

Another kind of Prolog program (like the BNA-project) applies Prolog as an executable approximation to declarative logic programming. The program is an explicit representation of the law and is *completely separated* from the deductive inference procedures. This fact is of great significance. The formalization of the BNA as Horn clauses is an axiomatic theory. Hence, any logical consequence of the axiomatization may, in theory, be derived by means of a complete mechanical theorem-prover. For this reason the Prolog formalization of a law may be used to assess the implications of the legislation or to help with some given legal problem relating to the law.

There is yet another advantage to the application of Logic Programming methods. Assume that during the process of drafting some (preliminary) act of law one formulates the draft as rules in Prolog-logic. It is then possible to use this formalization of the draft to derive various logical implications and consequences of the act, in a way similar to what may be done with an already valid piece of legislation (as discussed in section 3.2.2.2 with regard to the BNA).

Thus an executable, logic-based representation of rules and regulations may be used to aid the process of drafting and redrafting the rules in the first place, and not only after their acceptance and establishment of their authority. This idea was originally made by Allen in [Allen57]. He has later proposed that legislation should be drafted in a 'normalised' form based on logical connectives (see [Allen79]).

It may be argued that Prolog cannot deal with arbitrary sentences of logic. It is a special-purpose theorem-prover that is very efficient for proving certain kinds of simple theorems from axioms formulated as Horn clauses. But it sometimes goes into loops and fails to prove theorems that are logically implied by the axioms. Nevertheless, it can still be used to prove a large class of theorems and can help test a set of axioms by assisting in the derivation of logical consequences. Sergot discusses the adequacy of Prolog in [Sergot86] suggesting that many kinds of legislation can indeed be represented in Prolog, despite the fact that disjunctive conclusions are not allowed. He shows that also problems related to negated conditions in rules can usually be dealt with within the Prolog paradigm.

It is suggested that there are other potential advantages of representing rules and regulations in computer-executable logical form independent of the actual use of computers. Representation in logical form help to identify and eliminate unintended ambiguity and imprecision. It helps clarify and simplify the natural language statement of the rules themselves and therefore test them before they are put into force.

Let us elaborate this point by way of an example due to Layman E. Allen. Let us assume that the lending regulations in a university library has the following form[1] :

a. A separate form must be completed by the borrower for each volume borrowed.
b. Books should be returned by the date due.
c. Borrowers must not exceed their allowance of books on loan at any one time.
d. No book will be issued to borrowers who have books overdue for return to the library.

Book Allowances: Undergraduates 6   Academic staff 20   Postgraduates 10

Let us consider regulation b of this quasi-legal domain. The term 'should' lends itself (no pun intended) to several interpretations, of which we shall give a non-exhaustive list :

1. Books MAY, but NEED NOT be returned by the date due.

---

[1] These regulations have become part of the folklore of the AI and Law community. They form the Library Regulations for borrowing books at Imperial College, London. Their first appearance in the AI and Law literature is in [Sergot82]. As a former borrower from the Imperial College library I can assure the reader that the librarians there have absolutely no problem with the practical application of the rules. The reason for this is presumably that a unique interpretation has been accepted and adopted by all parties involved, librarians and borrowers.

2. Books MUST be returned by the date due.

3. The Borrower MAY, but NEED NOT return the books by the date due.

4. The borrower MUST return the books by the date due.

5. The borrower has DISCRETION with respect to the university of whether to return books by the date due.

6. The borrower has a DUTY to the university to return books by the date due.

7. The borrower has POWER to return books by the date due and MAY, but NEED NOT, exercise that power.

We have already pointed out that vagueness arising from open texture actually may increase the effectiveness of regulations (see section 1.6). The vagueness shown in the above rule due to *structural ambiguity* is of a different kind and should be eliminated if possible. Logic programming formalizations of legal rules may help towards that goal. For recent work on multiple structural interpretations of legal rules (as contrasted to semantic ambiguity, i.e. open texture) see [Allen89] and [Allen91]. We shall return to this kind of ambiguity at a later stage (see section 6.4.1).

We conclude this discussion of Logic Programming methods for statutory law systems by considering some implications relating to case-law. The advantages and suitability of Logic Programming claimed so far would also be applicable to case-law if it were possible to construct a logic-based representation for it. It is far from being obvious to which extent this could be done, as we saw in chapter two. While 'easy' cases may be resolved by using logical deduction this is not possible for 'hard' cases. Other workers have indeed used different approaches. We shall return to this issue at a later stage, and discuss to which extent case-law can be represented by Prolog-rules and how one can make use of these rules.

3.2.3 The TAXMAN I System.

3.2.3.1 Introduction.

The second system we shall survey is TAXMAN I, developed by L. Thorne McCarty in a project that started in 1972 and still continues (see section 3.5.1):

"The TAXMAN project is an experiment in the application of artificial intelligence to the study of legal reasoning and legal argumentation, using corporate tax law as an experimental domain." ([McCarty82]).

Our main interest is actually in the second part of the project, TAXMAN II, which focuses on open texture. It will be considered in section 3.5.1. The present discussion is restricted to TAXMAN I, a system for statutory law. It introduces the appropriate background and concepts, which appear in TAXMAN II. Besides, as we have already stated, knowledge and experience gained in the development of statutory-law systems may very well be of relevance also in case-law systems.

Concerning the first part of the project, a system (TAXMAN I) was developed, demonstrating:

"the possibility of constructing computer models of both the facts of corporate tax cases and the rules and concepts of the U.S. Internal Revenue Code and thus produce an analysis of the tax consequences of a given corporate transaction". ([McCarty77]).

3.2.3.2 U.S. Income Tax Law.

We shall first give a very brief introduction to the relevant area of statutory law, beginning with a hypothetical case given in [McCarty80], and based on United States v. Phellis, 257 U.S. 156 (1921). This will prepare the appropriate background for TAXMAN I, and allow us to indicate the difference between it and the concerns of TAXMAN II.

Assume there exists a New Jersey corporation which wishes to transfer its place of incorporation to Delaware in the following way. First, the New Jersey corporation (call it "New Jersey") sets up a new corporation in Delaware (call it "Delaware"), and transfers all its assets to Delaware in exchange for all of the newly issued Delaware stock. Second, New Jersey liquidates itself, and distributes the Delaware stock pro rata to its own stockholders in exchange for their original shares of New Jersey stock. The result of these two steps taken together is no more than a change in the state of incorporation, and the stockholders retain the same interest in the same operating assets as before.

Prior to 1918, the tax code imposed a potential tax liability on both the stockholders and the corporation in a case of this sort. Today, however, the Internal Revenue Code includes a series of "nonrecognition" and "basis" provisions for any transaction which fits within one of the six specified reorganization patterns (Internal Revenue Code, paragraph 368). As an indication of the complexity of this statute, here is the definition of a Type B reorganization:

"The acquisition by one corporation in exchange solely for all or a part of its voting stock (or in exchange solely for all or part of the voting stock of a corporation which is in control of the acquiring corporation), of stock of another corporation if, immediately after the acquisition, the acquiring corporation has control of such other corporation (whether or not such acquiring corporation had control immediately before the acquisition)."

Other related patterns include the Type C reorganization, which is an acquisition by one corporation in exchange "solely for ... voting stock" of "substantially all the properties" of another corporation.

We notice that our hypothetical case fits the general pattern of a Type C reorganization. Thus, under the the present statute, the two steps of our hypothetical case could be carried out tax free.

The TAXMAN I system is capable of representing and processing the precise rules of the Internal Revenue Code, such as the definition of a Type B reorganization, quoted above. It is capable of producing an analysis of the tax consequences of a given corporate transaction. For example the system is capable of representing the complete set of facts of United States v. Phellis, 257 U.S. 156 (1921) given above, and then classifying the case as a potential C-reorganization, though not a B-reorganization, since the New Jersey corporation's acquisition of control of the Delaware corporation was achieved in exchange for assets, rather than for voting stock ([McCarty77]).

3.2.3.3 Knowledge Representation.

TAXMAN I was originally implemented in micro-PLANNER and afterwards rewritten in the AIMDS representation language ([Sridharan78]).

The organization of the TAXMAN I model can be described by three levels. Quoting from [McCarty82]:

The "basic" facts of a corporate tax case can be represented in a relatively straightforward manner: corporations issue securities, transfer property, distribute dividends, etc. Below this level there is an expanded representation of the meaning of a security interest in terms of its component permissions and obligations: the owners of the shares of a common stock, for example, have certain rights to the "earnings", the "assets", and the "control" of the corporation. Above this level there is the "law": the statutory rules which classify transactions as taxable or non-taxable, ordinary income or capital gains, dividend distributions or stock redemptions, etc."

The basic knowledge representation structures are: templates, instances, relations and logical templates. *Templates* describe object-classes and *instances* of templates describe objects. For example, there may be a *template* expressing ownership of stock. An *instance* of this template could express the fact: "Phellis owns 100 shares of the New Jersey corporation". A *template* could describe corporations in general, while a specific *instance* could correspond to the New Jersey corporation. The *relations* are defined on or between the objects of the domain, e.g., owner or stock-quantity. A *logical template* defines concepts like "Type B reorganization".

Using this knowledge representation the TAXMAN I system is capable of analyzing the tax consequences of a given corporate transaction. This is carried out by *matching* a logical template to the facts of a case, and thus deciding whether the corresponding concept is true. As already mentioned in section 3.2.3.2 the system can represent the facts of the Phellis-case and classify it as a potential C reorganization.

3.2.3.4 The AXEMAN[2] System.

McCarty himself remarks that the knowledge representation of TAXMAN I is equivalent to Horn clause logic ([McCarty82]), and that the reasoning is essentially deductive ([McCarty83a]). We have developed a system equivalent to TAXMAN I , both in scope and functionality, but using methods of logic programming.

Our motivation for building this system was to confirm the possibility of reconstructing TAXMAN I in logical terms and also to gain a better understanding of TAXMAN II, to be described in section 3.5.1. A second reason, related to the first, was to develop conceptual knowledge structures in Prolog for the income tax domain. In section 3.3.4.3 we shall discuss what exactly is meant by conceptual knowledge structures. This domain was chosen by McCarty to illustrate his model for open texture. We considered the possibility of actually implementing a system dealing with open texture in this area. The reasons why we eventually decided against such an implementation will be dealt with later.

The formalization of the relevant income tax law contains not more than ten rules, while the conceptual structures (common stock, cumulative debenture notes etc.) are represented as binary relationships (see [Kowalski79], p.33).

Thus a Type C reorganization (represented in TAXMAN I as a logical template) would essentially be represented by the following rule:

---

[2] The name AXEMAN indicates the roots of the system in TAXMAN, and also expresses what many consider the main function of the Internal Revenue Collector.

reorganization-type-C

iff	exchange n1 n2
and	transferor(n1, CORPORATION)
and	transferor(n2 , CORPORATION)
and	transfer-object(n1, common_stock)
and	transfer-object (n2, property_assets).

Here n1 and n2 are variables representing entities executing an exchange. The entities must be CORPORATIONS (see below) and one entity transfers common stock while the other one transfers property.

A data-item of type CORPORATION (represented in TAXMAN I as a template-instance) would be defined by a set of assertions, as follows:

```
isa (<item> CORPORATION)
name (<item> <constant>)
time (<item> <constant>)
common_stock_authorized (<item> <constant>)
COMMON_STOCK (<item> <constant>)
PREFERRED_STOCK (<item> <constant>)
cash-assets (<item> <constant>)
property_assets (<item> <constant>)
etc.
```

This set of definitions asserts that <item> is a Corporation, gives its name and the time when the assertions are valid. Next appears the amount of authorized stock, the actual amount of issued common stock and issued preferred stock. Finally the assertions give the amount of cash-assets of the corporation, the amount of property-assets. Other kinds of shares or bonds are indicated by et cetera.

Our conclusion from the experience of this implementation is obvious. TAXMAN I could indeed be reconstructed as a deductive system using Prolog logic. Concerning the lack of treatment of open texture, the observations made about the BNA project can here be repeated in almost unchanged form. The slight change arises from the different approach of TAXMAN I to input of data. The conclusions, however, are the same. There is no difference in principle between querying:

"Does New Jersey transfer all its assets (to Delaware)? Please answer yes or no" or adding an assertion (or its negation) of the form:

transfer-object(New-Jersey, property-assets).

Hence, we can state that the TAXMAN I system ignores the open texture of the law either in the formalization of the tax code itself or through the input of the basic facts which lack a consideration of open texture. Alternatively, as we pointed out in section 3.2.2.2 with respect to the BNA program, we can consider the system as expressing open texture, but only being applicable for 'easy' cases.

These problems of open texture motivated McCarty in undertaking the TAXMAN II project. In this project he attempts to develop a computational theory of legal reasoning which directly addresses open texture. Such a theory tries to explain how a judge will reach a decision in a new case reasoning about previous precedents, and it attempts to simulate the legal argumentation of the judge in reaching this decision.

Further implications of the TAXMAN I project will be given in chapter four.

3.3 Jurimetrics.

3.3.1 Introduction.

The foundations of the field of jurimetrics may be traced back to an article by Lee Loevinger ([Loevinger49]). He proposes the creation of a new area relating to both law and science:

The next step forward in the long path of man's progress must be from jurisprudence (which is mere speculation about law) to jurimetrics - which is the scientific investigation of legal problems" ([Loevinger49], p.483).

Thus, taken in the broadest sense, jurimetrics would include any use of scientific methods and tools, among them also computers, for the purpose of dealing with legal issues. Therefore any computer application to law, specifically the investigation and building of legal computer systems for case-law could be considered a topic in jurimetrics.

However, the field is commonly considered as having a narrower extent. It is usually taken to include three main topics:

(1) Behavioural analysis and prediction of the actions of witnesses, lawyers, judges, legislators etc.
(2) The use of logic in law.
(3) Legal information retrieval.

Sometimes the word jurimetrics is used to denote the first area only. However, we shall use it in an intermediate sense, and consider each of the three areas defined above. This is really a matter of convenience. Many of the issues in these areas are related to the problem of building a computer system for case-law, but do not appear naturally in any other context.

3.3.2 Behavioural Aspects.

A motive for considering and developing this area is supplied by Loevinger himself:

"Much, and perhaps most, of the uncertainty in legal prediction arises from the inability to forecast what the facts will be, or what the courts will infer them to be from the evidence, or even what the evidence will be upon trial. ([Loevinger61], p.268).

Loevinger does not make use of the concept of open texture. However, it seems clear that the reason we cannot forecast what the facts will be, or what the courts will infer them to be, is precisely because of the open texture of law.

He suggests that one way to attack this problem of uncertainty is through the application of statistics. One may apply methods commonly used in the Social Sciences and, for example, analyse previous decisions by individual judges. Much research has been done on this subject, and an overview may be found in [Lawlor80].

A related approach is to utilize the knowledge of an expert lawyer in the particular area of law to be dealt with. He would draw upon his experience to evaluate evidence of a given case. He would know how this evidence should be submitted to the court, and how it probably would be interpreted by the judge. To this end the expert would also have knowledge about the 'track-record' of individual judges.

These approaches would be important features in the building of an experiential system, but would not contribute to an academic system.

3.3.3 Methods of Logic.

Most jurists agree that there are certain elements of logic in legal reasoning, most obvious in the use of logical deduction. However, the use of logic in law is more extensive. In section 3.2.2.3 we have already mentioned the use of logic in analysing legislation or drafts of legislation. Many expert systems in law may be classified as deductive, rule-based, and most certainly make use of logic. Indeed, one of our objects in discussing the BNA project (in section 3.2.2) was to consider the use of logic programming methods in (statutory) law.

Major parts of this book deal with deductive systems, so we shall here only consider one application of logic to law, the so-called deontic logic. We consider this topic as it happens to be connected with the theories of Hohfeld, which we described in chapter two. It appears that this theoretical topic has some relation to the building of legal computer systems.

In 1951 vonWright introduced the concept of deontic logic, or logic of normative concepts in [vonWright51]. He further developed the theory, which originally had no special connection with law, in [vonWright63]. The word 'deontic' is derived from a Greek word meaning 'as it should be' or 'duly'.

The object of deontic logic is to construct formal theories of the various normative concepts and also to test the adequacy of these theories by applying them to the analysis of ethical discussion. We shall here only outline the basic ideas, so as to establish the connection with the work of Hohfeld.

The basic normative concepts studied in deontic logic include 'obligation', 'duty', permission', 'right' and related expressions. Assume, for example, that p denotes any action or state of affairs. Assume that 'p is permitted' is expressed as P p, and 'p is obligatory' as O p. Furthermore, let $\neg$ denote negation. Then the following relation is true:

$$O p = \neg P(\neg p).$$

vonWright adopts a number of axioms relating to these normative concepts. To this he adds the customary rules of inference from propositional logic. He also defines the following rule:"if actions or state of affairs p and q are logically equivalent, the Pp and Pq are also logically equivalent". Here P is as defined above.

When the normative concepts like 'permission' and 'obligation' are given a legal interpretation it is possible to apply deontic logic to legal analysis. It is possible to establish a direct connection between deontic concepts and the basic concepts ('right', 'duty' etc.) introduced by Hohfeld and described in section 2.3.3 (see [Kanger71]). For another effort to analyse law using Hohfeldian concepts see [Allen86].

A computer system incorporating Hohfeldian concepts has been constructed for case-law. The system, STARE (see [Goldman87]), is best classified as a conceptual retrieval system (see 3.3.4.3).

The use of deontic logic in computer system is also considered in [McCarty83] and [McCarty86], but in a way which is not directly relevant to our topic. Bench-Capon argues in [Bench89] that there is no need for deontic logic in computer systems for the routine application of law. We shall return to his argumentation in section 4.3.2.

3.3.4 Legal Case Retrieval.

3.3.4.1 Introduction.

In this section we shall consider a number of projects and methods from the area of document information retrieval. This area is related to the problems that arise in case-law computer systems, as information retrieval systems, among other things, also are concerned with retrieval of *cases*. In the introduction (section 1.1) we briefly mentioned methods of document retrieval which were based upon the appearance of certain keywords - or combinations of keywords - in the retrieved documents. In the following we shall discuss some of the other methods applied in this area, which perhaps are more appropriate for legal systems.

One method deals with the retrieval of cases based on certain statistical features of the documents (the vector method). It could perhaps be useful in an experiential system. The other method deals with conceptual retrieval and is directly related to our subject, as it may be used in an academic computer system. Such systems, in fact, exist and will also be considered.

3.3.4.2 Vector Methods.

3.3.4.2.1 General method.

The problem we shall consider is the following: Given a database of documents (e.g. law-reports) and given a new document (describing the facts of a new case), how do we retrieve those documents from the database which are most 'similar' in some sense to the given, new document.

The vector method, developed by Salton (see e.g. [Salton83]) does not attempt to show whether certain documents *are* or *are not* relevant to a given new one. This is done by the classical methods using appearance of keywords. Instead this method tells us that they are *more* or *less* relevant.

Each document is represented by a vector of term-weights. The terms, which determine the number of elements of the vectors are commonly the words (or word-forms) appearing in the document database. Not all the words appearing are chosen, but only a subset of words characteristic of the documents. There are also other possibilities for defining terms, as we shall see below. For a given document the weights are chosen according to some statistical scheme, so that a positive weight signifies that the corresponding term appears in the document, while the weight is zero if the term does not appear in the document. The term-weight is assumed to measure the importance of the appearance of the relevant term in the document.[3]

Consider now a new document (perhaps describing the facts of a case and its decision) with its associated vector. Our object is to retrieve 'similar' documents from the database. One approach would be is to insist upon a *complete match* between all non-zero terms of this vector and the vector of a document we may want to retrieve. In this case two documents would either match completely (i.e. be considered similar) or not match at all (i.e. not be considered similar). Instead, Salton's method defines a similarity measure between the vector of weights of the document at hand and each vector corresponding to a document in the database. The greater the measure the more 'similar' is the retrieved document to the given document.[4] It is now possible to define a certain threshold. As retrieved documents we can consider those for whom the computed similarity measure is greater than the threshold.

3.3.4.2.2   Nearest   Neighbours.

An application of the vector method to law was developed for the DataLex project. This project described in [Greenleaf87] has a component which attempts "to simulate the

---

[3] A possible weight-scheme for words would define the value of a weight as the relative frequency of the word, i.e. the number of appearances of the word divided by the total number of words in the document.

[4] The correlation between two vectors is often defined by the so-called 'cosine measure'. This defined as the scalar product of the vectors divided by the product of their lengths.

reasoning used by lawyers when dealing with case-law" ([Greenleaf87], p.13). To that end it uses a method for retrieving cases, that we shall now describe. The system has a case-base in the area of law which governs the right of possession of chattels which have been lost or abandoned.

The user is queried by the system to determine the weights of the legally significant parameters (in the terminology of the previous section: the 'terms') for a new case to be considered. These significant parameters have been predefined by the implementators, who have also assigned weights to all document vectors in the given case-database. The system can then retrieve the 'nearest neighbour' of the case at hand, i.e. the case from the database which together with the given case yields the largest similarity measure.

[Greenleaf87] does not give many details about the system, and there are no concrete examples of what the legally significant parameters are in the given area of application.

We shall briefly report the actual use of the retrieved 'nearest neighbour' case. The authors consider this case the 'most persuasive' and the most likely to be followed. The system also advises which of the cases is 'most likely to support a contrary decision'. This is presumably that case in the database which has a contrary decision and together with the case at hand yields the largest similarity measure. This is, however, not stated specifically in the paper. The final output is a report which describes the most persuasive case, states the similar features and also the points where this case differs from the case at hand. Also the case most likely to support a contrary decision is described, stating the features which correspond to the case at hand and also the dissimilar features.

The authors assert that the system may be used as a tool for solving what they call the 'discretion problem', i.e., what we have called the problem of 'hard' cases:

"although it seems likely that a completely successful system must call on the expert author to assign subjective weighing to the attributes which could be used in a probabilistic way to judge the reliability of the final advice." ([Greenleaf87], p.14).

In chapter four we shall return to this method. We shall then discuss the propriety of using the method and also consider what weight a 'most persuasive' case may have in a legal argument.

3.3.4.2.3 Citation Vectors.

Tapper points out some drawbacks of Salton's vector method as applied to words

([Tapper80]). Instead he proposes to use the vector method to the citations appearing in the documents. For case-reports the citations include reference to statutes and decisions of previous cases.

In Tappers opinion it is very difficult to determine the appropriate words (not to mention their synonyms) defining the terms of the vectors in the original vector method. It appears that a user has difficulty deciding which words characteristically express the meaning of a document. Another problem with terms defined as words is related to the fact that words have shades of meaning. They can be used indirectly and metaphorically, and they acquire meaning by position, emphasis and association. This of course decreases the reliability of retrieval according to words.

In view of these difficulties Tapper proposes to use citations instead of words. By citation he means the *fact* of reference and not the *notation* of such a reference. What complicates the matter is that there exist competing series of law-reports, so that a given case may be designated by any one of a large number of possible different forms of notation, which should all be regarded as equivalent.

The advantages of the method as stated by Tapper are as follows:

(1) The notation is short; It conveys the meaning of thousands of words in a few symbols.
(2) "Man bites dog" and "Dog bites man" have different meanings, not detected in the classical vector method. Reference within a document to two sources has the same meaning whatever the order of citation to these sources.
(3) Citations have a number of parameters not possessed by words, for example dimensions of age and juristic status in the sense of being applied, doubted, followed, distinguished or overruled.
(4) They also have a parameter common with words, namely the frequency of occurrence.

For a more recent application of citations see [Merkl90].

The retrieval method outlined here is different from the the one previously considered (in 3.3.4.2.2). However, the same questions concerning its applicability in an academic advisory system may be raised.

We shall now proceed to methods whose object is to retrieve cases, but they go about it in such a way that they can be considered advisory systems in themselves. These are the 'conceptual retrieval' systems.

3.3.4.3 Conceptual Retrieval.

The term "conceptual retrieval" has been used by several researchers: "to refer to systems that index and retrieve information using *conceptual structures* rather than *text structures*" ([Hafner87], p.35). For example, in a text retrieval system we may search for the concept of "enjoyment", which often appears in nuisance cases in the form: "enjoyment of land", but also may appear alone as "enjoyment". This concept could be related to words like: pleasure, comfort, ease etc. Now these words could also be used to describe other kinds of feelings which have no bearing upon nuisance. A text retrieval system would therefore retrieve not only relevant documents, but also some where one of these words was used in an entirely different sense. On the other hand, consider a document where a judge in a pollution-case is quoted as saying: "A neighbour is entitled to breathe fresh and clean air". This document would *not* be retrieved by a classical retrieval system looking for "enjoyment of land" or synonyms thereof despite the fact that it is very relevant. A conceptual system would explicitly contain a *concept*: "enjoyment of land" so that all and only those documents that pertain to "enjoyment of land" could be retrieved - no matter how the concept is described in the documents.

The paradigm of Case-Based Reasoning (CBR) was described in section 1.7. We may consider conceptual retrieval as being the first steps of CBR.

An early work on conceptual retrieval was [Hafner78], which was later published in book-form as [Hafner81]. The legal domain selected by Hafner consists of Articles 3 and 4 of the Uniform Commercial Code (in USA), which are the provisions governing negotiable instruments such as cheques and notes. In Hafner's system, called LIRS, it is possible to retrieve cases relating to concepts like 'forged indorsement' or 'plaintiff is not a holder in due course'.

For a more recent approach to the subject of conceptual retrieval see [Hafner87], which we shall follow closely below.

One way to approach conceptual retrieval, as proposed by Hafner, is to discover the methods legal experts use in remembering and classifying cases. These methods may then be implemented in a computer system.

To that end one may define two components of the system:

(1) "Domain knowledge" which defines the range of concepts the system will understand: The actors, events and relationships.
(2) Algorithms for matching concept descriptions for retrieval purposes.

The domain knowledge is utilized by the matching algorithms, so that if a particular concept is required, the system will retrieve not only that exact concept but all closely related concepts.

The domain knowledge may be represented according to different formal methods (semantic networks, logic programs etc.). All these methods provide the following knowledge structures:

(1) Taxonomic hierarchies for defining relations among objects. For example common-stock (in the TAXMAN domain) is a kind of security, cash is a kind of corporate asset.

(2) Role structures which define important situations. For example a corporate reorganization has a *transferor* and a *transferee*.

(3) Decision rule hierarchies specify under which conditions a concept is true or false. As an example we may consider the set of Prolog rules defining a C-reorganization in section 3.2.3.4.

Using domain knowledge of the above structure a program may now retrieve cases in a given area of law. Hafner makes an important remark concerning such a retrieval. Assume a lawyer is dealing with a nuisance case. He knows that 'reasonable activity' is a good defence and may attempt to retrieve cases relating to this concept. However, there are other good defences not involving 'reasonable activity' at all. Cases giving decisions related to those other defences should perhaps also be retrieved.

For that purpose ("navigating" through the case-base, as she refers to it) Hafner proposes the use of an *issue/case discrimination tree*. The nodes of the tree are of two kinds: issue-nodes and factor-nodes. Issues are the concepts the case deals with which are decided by the case. Factors are considerations which may influence the decision of an issue.

Each node has a link to the case law collection. This link points to a set of cases in which the particular issue or factor was important. Hafner does not deal with the problem of building the issue/factor tree. Nor does she explain how the links to the case-sets are to be established.

For other recent work on conceptual retrieval see [Bing87], [Bing89] and [Gelbart91].

Of the various retrieval methods discussed until now only conceptual retrieval appears to be directly related to *academic* systems. As a matter of fact, a conceptual retrieval system may be considered an academic advisory system. For given the facts of a case the system will retrieve the relevant cases and their decisions. In 'hard' cases this is anyway all we can aim at. Hafner's proposal for retrieving cases is similar to the approach used in HYPO (see section 3.4.3) and **JURIX**. We shall make a comparison of the methods in chapter four.

3.4 Case Law Systems.

We have so far considered various subjects and research projects that all had some bearing upon our topic: computer systems for case-law. We chose these topics because they throw some light upon the nature of open texture or because they dealt with case-law, but from somewhat different angles or with different objects in mind. Time has now come to consider the small number of computer systems which in the past have directly addressed the issues of case-law. The first of these systems, by Meldman, attempts to compare cases through analogy and generalization. The second system, by Gardner, actually addresses problems of open texture and case-law and is thus directly relevant to our work. The third system, HYPO (by Rissland and Ashley) is an advisory system, which retrieves cases relevant to a given one and attempts to deal with the selection and weighing of these precedents. We shall also consider another system by Rissland (and Skalak) called CABARET, and a system by Branting called GREBE. They are both hybrid systems, i.e., systems applying both rule-based and case-based reasoning.

Such systems could consider historical development, social and economic aspects of the law etc. This would make their task extremely formidable. As a matter of fact all the systems are concerned only with the analysis component of legal reasoning. Even then they face many very difficult problems. We shall see below how they deal with these problems, and in the next chapter we shall evaluate their various approaches to a solution.

3.4.1 Meldman's System.

3.4.1.1 Introduction.

Meldman in [Meldman75] describes a computer system for dealing with cases relating to the torts of assault and battery. It was supposed to be a prototype for a computer system that can perform 'a simple kind of legal analysis' ([Meldman75], p.9). To that end he constructs a model for representing factual situations and legal knowledge. We shall describe this model and Meldman's kind of analysis below.

By legal analysis Meldman means: "the logical derivation of a legal conclusion from a particular factual situation in the light of some body of legal doctrine". He distinguishes this from legal reasoning, or rather considers it as "the logical component of legal reasoning". The relevant body of legal doctrine he takes to be statutes (and constitutions) and case-law. By logical derivation he means 'logic of syllogism' (applying rules to facts by deduction) and analogy.

Meldman devotes space in his thesis to some background on legal analysis and legal reasoning. He also discusses legal information retrieval, but there is no consideration of the important developments of theories of law and legal reasoning during the last 50-60 years. The concept of open texture is nowhere mentioned.

The program was designed to be executed by a system called OWL (see [Szolovits77]), which was not implemented. Later, King implemented a system based on Meldman's design which put more emphasis on the analogy-mechanism ([King76]).

A logic program which deals with the same area of law was later built by Hustler ([Hustler82]). Hustler derived his rules from the same text-book on torts used by Meldman: [Prosser41]. As he did not address the issue of case-law reasoning, we shall not consider his work any more.

3.4.1.2 Background and Implementation.

In order to describe Meldman's model consider first the definition of assault, according to [Prosser41], p.48:

"The defendant is liable for the apprehension of immediate harmful or offensive contact with the defendant's person, caused by acts intended to result in such contacts, or the apprehension of them, directed at the plaintiff or a third person."

Meldman observes that this can be written as a logical proposition. He points out that in some models this proposition would be represented in one indivisible chunk, as the models may not be able to represent factual pieces like 'apprehension', 'offensive contact' and 'defendant'. Meldman's aim is to build a structural model from small factual pieces and a large assortment of relations, so that it will be possible by a mechanical procedure to determine whether or not a given factual situation matches the situation that the proposition represents. He remarks that it is not obvious how much decomposability of concepts one should aim at. We shall return to that interesting issue in the next chapter.

Meldman chooses a structural model in which matching of factual pieces can be carried out at various levels. At the lowest level the matching is accomplished by arranging the facts in a hierarchy of categories, called the kind-hierarchy. At higher levels the matching is accomplished in terms of structures of factual pieces.

Meldman's legal sources are a fictious collection of rules: Corpus Juris Mechanicum (extracted from [Prosser41]), and a set of five cases with their decisions, four of which are for the plaintiff, and one for the defendant.

As an example of the legal rules we shall state the following rule defining battery, which for simplicity we have rephrased in a propositional form:

Battery **if** Plaintiff **and** Defendant **and** Contact **and** Intent **and** Lack of Consent.

This is followed by further definitions of Contact, Intent etc. according to the legal definition of battery as given by [Prosser41] (p.43):

"One is liable to another for unpermitted, unprivileged contacts with his person, caused by acts intended to result in such contacts, or the apprehension of them, directed at the other or a third person".

Meldman represents the set of cases by a set of rules each stating a fixed ratio decidendi. As an example we shall rephrase one such rule in propositional form:

contact   **iff**   foe-v-moe-situation
foe-v-moe-situation   **iff**   one person strikes another in the anatomy

The rule here is a generalization of what is given in the actual example, Foe v. Moe. This generalization is carried out by the implementator. In the case Foe v. Moe, Joe Moe actually punched Fred Foe in the nose. The ratio defined in the system uses *strike* as a generalization of *punch* and *anatomy* as a generalization of *nose*.

The system uses classical forms for knowledge representation: semantic networks and structures resembling frames. A structure corresponding to the above rule will contain a slot pointing to the actual precedent (Foe-v-Moe) and the specific facts of that case.

The rule defining battery (actually derived from [Prosser41]) is assumed to be the ratio of a fictious case: Smith-v-Jones. In other words, the legal knowledge of the system (the rationes) may be represented in the form of propositional rules, each of them linked to a (real or fictious) case it is supposedly derived from. These rules are what Susskind denotes case-law statements.

In order to explain the working of Meldman's system consider an example given by Meldman (p. 184):

"Aaron Aardvark purposely kicked Zachary Zetz in the leg."

The system will attempt to apply the ratio of the (fictious) case: Smith v. Jones, i.e. the rule defining battery. It will first attempt to prove the separate components: Contact and Intent.

In order to prove Contact it will apply the rule given previously: contact **iff** foe-v-moe-situation etc. To that end it must consider the concepts *kicked* and *leg*. The system contains a generalization and analogy hierarchy which may now be applied. From the generalization hierarchy the program discovers that *strike* is a generalization of *kick*, and *anatomy* is a generalization of *leg*. This enables the program to conclude Contact. The Intent component is concluded in a similar way from the fact that Aardvark kicked Zetz *purposely*.

After succeeding in establishing Intent the system must prove Lack of Consent. As there is no successful instantiation with one of the given cases the system queries the user:

"Did Zachary Zetz consent to being kicked?"

The natural language interface for the system was not implemented, so the above question is actually the English translation of what the program really asks. If the user answers No, the system will conclude that Aaron Aardvark is liable to Zachary Zetz for a battery.

We shall consider yet another example which illustrates another feature of the system. It is also given by Meldman (p.191):

"With the purpose of frightening Gordon Good, Howard Hood visibly points a saturday-night special at him and grabs the umbrella that he is holding. The saturday-night special is not loaded."

The term "saturday-night special" is not known to the system. By querying the user it is informed that a saturday-night special is a kind of pistol, a term found in the kind-hierarchy.

As in the previous example the system will attempt to instantiate Contact. It will encounter the case Roe v. Doe, another one of the five build-in cases (which we have not described before). The generalized rule from Roe v. Doe holds that striking of an *article of clothing* on a person is sufficient to establish Contact. According to the kind-hierarchy an *umbrella* is not an *article of clothing*, but a *personal accessory*. However, an article of clothing is an **analog** of a personal accessory, for they are both kinds of *movable objects*. Similarly *grab* is an **analog** of *strike*, as they are both kinds of *contact-events*.

After succeeding in establishing Intent (which follows from the use of the word 'purpose') the system must prove Lack of Consent. As in the previous example the system queries the user whether Good consented to the grabbing of his umbrella. If the user answers No, the system will conclude that Howard Hood is liable to Gordon Good for a battery.

The output of the system is a Yes/No answer, and the program can show the reasoning (logical deduction) leading to such an answer, emphasizing the deduction steps assumed a priori by the user.

The main features of Meldman's system may be summarized as follows: Battery and Assault are defined by general rules relating to concepts like Contact, Intent etc. These general rules are assumed to be the ratio of a fictious case, Smith v. Jones. The precedents are also represented in the system by generalized rules. For example, Contact (as in Foe v. Moe) is 'when one person strikes another in the anatomy'. A new case is defined by basic facts ('Hood grabbed umbrella') and the system attempts to fit these basic facts to the general rules by using the generalization and analogy hierarchy.

If a component of battery or assault, for example Intent, cannot be proved the system queries the user directly as to the validity of this feature. Also the input of an object not recognized by the kind-hierarchy (as e.g. saturday-night special) will raise a query.

3.4.1.3   Discussion.

Meldman himself does not mention the concept of open texture, but obviously the issue is treated within the system. We shall now consider how.

We have already explained that Meldman creates a general rule for each case stored in the case-base, i.e. a case-law statement, while the facts of the case are kept for documentary purposes only. The facts of a new case are subsumed directly or by analogy/generalization with respect to the set of rules.

Meldman's system is thus a case-law system using the rule-based approach. Now this set of rules is quite similar to a set of statutes. We may therefore describe Meldman's model as a statutory-law system + analogy/generalization. The treatment of open texture is similar to the one described in the section on the BNA system (section 3.2.2.2) as we shall now explain.

It is possible to look at this treatment in three ways:

1. The formulation of the general rules arising from the given cases ignores completely the open texture of the (case)-law.

2. The formulation of the general rules expresses the open texture, but the rigid use of the predefined kind-hierarchy lacks any consideration of it. For there could conceivably be cases where there were reasons to consider *kick* as a kind of *strike*, and also reasons for **not** considering it so.

3. The system can be applied only in 'easy' cases, where the use of the kind-hierarchy is obviously correct and the rules themselves are clearly relevant to the case.

Meldman's system raises many interesting points relating to the problem of common-sense knowledge, the use of analogy/generalization and his approach to legal reasoning in general. In the following chapter (chapter four) we shall consider these issues.

3.4.2 Gardner's Work.

3.4.2.1   Introduction.

Modern jurisprudential theories raise many relevant questions and problems for people who build legal expert systems. The work by A. Gardner to be described in this section ([Gardner84]) is characterized by an approach which attempts to incorporate such jurisprudential theory. A revised version of Gardner's thesis has been published in book-form ([Gardner87]).

Gardner's aim was to: "create a model of the legal reasoning process that makes sense from both jurisprudential and AI perspectives." Specifically she wanted to address the problems of open texture and the application of case-law. This is of course directly relevant to our topic. Her system attempted to distinguish 'easy' cases from 'hard' ones, and reach a level of sophistication where it could answer exam-questions from courses in the legal area she chose (contract-law, specifically problems of offer-and-acceptance). From an AI point of view there was an aspect related to the understanding of natural language dialogue. The system is implemented in MRS (see [Genesereth84]).

In the Anglo-American legal system contract-law is an area of case-law. In order for a contract to be valid several elements must usually be present. Among those elements Gardner concentrates on two central features:

(1) An *offer* (by a party called the offeror).
(2) An *acceptance* of the offer (by a party called the offeree).

Besides case-reports Gardner makes use of the Restatement of Contracts ([Restatement81]). The Restatement is an attempt to formulate the rules of contract law. It is unofficial in the sense that it has no formal legal authority. However, it is very influential as judges and lawyers quote it and use it in their deliberations.

Given the facts of a case it is often not clear whether an offer in fact was made and by whom. Not every offer (in the everyday sense) is an offer in the legal sense, and the formulation, time and medium of communication are relevant issues. The offeree may sometimes give a *counteroffer* in reply to an offer. Such a counteroffer of course requires an acceptance by the original offeror, etc.

As Gardner points out herself, the selected legal area has some features in common with Meldman's choice of assault and battery. It is an area dominated by case-law and is taught early in law-school, so that not much other legal knowledge is prerequisite. There is an additional feature which also is characteristic of Meldman's area: The major dependence on common-sense knowledge. However, contract-law differs from assault and battery in being centrally concerned with interpreting what people have said one to another. This problem and the related problem of understanding language dialogues combine with the legal problems such a system must deal with.

The program accepts as input a list of events to be accounted for. The system then attempts to characterize each event as defining an offer, an acceptance or a counteroffer. In hard questions it may be impossible to find a best characterization, and the output consists therefore of a tree. Each node corresponds to an event and each arc corresponds to either an offer, an acceptance or a counteroffer. Each path from the root of the tree to a leaf corresponds to a distinct analysis and interpretation of the case. For easy cases the program supplies an actual decision. For hard cases it will discover the fact that the case is hard but do no further processing.

3.4.2.2 Representation and Utilization of Legal Knowledge.

In order to represent the specification of events over time, Gardner defines a network similar to an augmented transition network (ATN). This is the *first class of legal knowledge*. The states are elements of a space of *possible* legal relations (One or more offers are pending, a contract exists, etc.). The arcs of the network correspond to events that can change the legal relations between the parties. They can be labeled 'offer', 'acceptance', 'counteroffer', 'rejection' etc.

The *second class of legal knowledge* is a class of rules which deals with how to recognize these basic legal categories. The source of these rules is [Restatement81]. For example:

Section 24. Offer Defined.

An offer is the manifestation of willingness to enter into a bargain, so made as to justify another person in understanding that his assent to that bargain is invited and will conclude it.

The English sentence: "Buyer sent Seller a telegram" will be represented in MRS by a set of assertions here written in general logical form:

send (Send1)
agent (Send1 Buyer)
object (Send1 Telegram1)
telegram (Telegram1)

An offer-and-acceptance problem may then be defined by a sequence of events each described by a statement of the above form.

The MRS language uses a predicate-calculus syntax, and each factual case may therefore be described by a set of assertions. The unary predicates are used in a predefined hierarchy, which Gardner does not always represent in predicate-calculus syntax, though the formalism is quite clear.

For example:

Legal-act
      Offer
            Counteroffer
            Offer-to-modify
            Modification-of-offer
      Acceptance
      Rejection
      Revocation

Gardner deals with the question of level of detail in the problem representation:

"If the problem speaks of supplying something, it may be unnecessary to ask what further facts - perhaps about shipment and delivery - constitute this supplying. Providing predicates at various levels of abstraction, then, seems to make for a relatively economical, relatively natural initial problem representation." (p. 94)

We shall return to the issue raised here, i.e. at what level of detail the program should operate, in the next chapter.

There is also a *third class of legal knowledge*, which relates to the knowledge-base of cases. We shall now discuss this aspect of the knowledge representation.

Gardner first mentions the possibility of giving a *detailed factual representation* of each case, but discards it for two reasons.

1. Stating what the facts are is a matter of interpretation. The only way to avoid a misinterpretation is to reproduce the law-report literally. This would be appropriate when using the approach of full text information systems but not in the kind of advisory system Gardner discusses.

2. Gardner argues that the kind of representation that, e.g. is proposed by [Hafner87] is very complex and does not contribute to the kind of system she has built, i.e., a system which supplies answers for 'easy' cases and diagnoses 'hard' ones.

In order to see this, Gardner observes that for any given predicate one may expect to find many cases silently treating the satisfaction of this predicate as an 'easy' question. For example a precedent in contract-law may deal with some problem concerning the *acceptance* of an offer, assuming that the offer itself is legally valid. When dealing with legal problems of *offers*, there would therefore be no need to retrieve such a case. When dealing with 'hard' legal problems of *acceptance* the case could be retrieved to supply an argument for a certain court-decision, while another case dealing with acceptance could be retrieved to supply a reason for the opposite decision. Thus, for the purpose of disposing efficiently of 'easy' questions *only*, there is no need for the factual representation of the cases. The fact that the case is easy means precisely that it can be decided by a rule. Hence, it is sufficient to supply such rules and not complicated case-descriptions.

Instead of using factual representation of cases, Gardner proposes to use a set of what she calls 'fact patterns' associated with each legal predicate. A pattern is a rule. It may be supported by several cases, and a case may contribute to several such patterns. An example of such a pattern would be the rule:

manifestation **iff** message-by-telegram

There are, however, several differences between the legal rules described previously and patterns.
(1) The patterns are understood to use everyday language, while the previous rules are understood to use only legal predicates.
(2) The patterns are not intended to exhaust the possibilities. This is a very important point to be considered below.
(3) The patterns may be inconsistent. One case may treat a given predicate as obviously satisfied, while another case may treat it as obviously not satisfied.
(4) The patterns are context dependent. Thus it can be taken into account that it is one question whether a bicycle is a 'vehicle' within a rule prohibiting vehicles in a park, while it is a separate question whether it falls within the requirement that vehicles travel on the left-hand side of the road (at least in the U.K.).

It is not clear from Gardner's description how she derives these patterns. It seems correct to consider some of them as case-law statements, some of them as law-specializations and others as law-generalizations.

Given a specific case, one may try to approach it using the knowledge structures and rules described so far. However, Gardner explains that this would fail to deal with the issues she wants to address. In section 3.2.2.2. we saw that applying rules has three interpretations: (1) The rules ignore open texture, (2) The rules express the open texture, but the assumption of definite (yes/no) answers concerning the validity of the rules ignores the open texture, and (3) Because of the assumption of definite answers the rules are applicable in 'easy' cases only. Gardner raises a fourth possibility:
(4) Assume that the rules express the open texture, there is no 'right' answer, i.e. there is no capability of giving definite answers, and thus all cases are 'hard'.

Assuming that all cases are 'easy' is an oversimplification. Similarly, assuming that all cases are 'hard' does not give a very useful system. Thus, if one assumes the fourth approach (cases are 'hard'), one would need an additional feature to distinguish which cases nevertheless ought to be 'easy'.

Such an additional feature is supplied by the so-called CSK rules to be discussed in the next section.

3.4.2.3   Common Sense Knowledge Representation.

The CSK-rules (common-sense knowledge rules) are expressed in MRS. They enable the system to decide that some cases will be easy. They can do this in one of three ways.

1. They may express the fact that a certain concept belongs to 'the core of certainty' and not to the 'penumbra of doubt'. For example, if a legal rule states that something has to be done within a *reasonable time* a CSK-rule could help the system conclude that an action carried out 'immediately' indeed was carried out 'in reasonable time'.

2. A legal concept may have a meaning too far removed from everyday usage to have an intuitive meaning. The CSK-rules could help to provide knowledge about everyday situations covered by these legal concepts. For example, if A writes to B: "I hereby offer to sell you my car for $1000" the CSK-rules may help deciding that this is 'a manifestation of willingness to enter into a bargain'.

3. Sometimes the usual interpretation of facts will lead to the mistaken conclusion that the case is easy. The CSK-rules may help defeat such an erroneous inference.

The execution of the program now proceeds as follows. Gardner first applies the general rules (derived from the Restatement), and the CSK rules. A concept may have a definition both according to the technical-legal rules and according to the non-technical

CSK-rules. In such a case the technical definition is usually preferred.

If the knowledge of the program is insufficient to conclude whether a certain rule is true or false, the patterns may help fill in gaps in this knowledge. If at a certain stage *competing* rules are encountered, they are all applied. If they agree at each stage of the execution, it means that the concepts involved which express the open texture all have exact, previous definitions. The outcome of the case is deduced by the system, and the case is judged 'easy'. If, however, all the knowledge sources taken together provide no answer, or if at any stage competing rules yield different results in the case being analyzed, the choice between them is considered to raise a 'hard' question. The significance is that different approaches to the legal analysis exist, and no further processing takes place.

3.4.2.4 Understanding Dialogues.

In the area of contract-law a program must be able to represent and reason about statements like:

"Will you supply carload of salt at $2.40 per cwt?"

or:

"Accept your offer carload of salt, immediate shipment, terms cash on delivery."

A substantial part of Gardner's thesis is devoted to representation and understanding of speech acts and their legal significance. In the area of contracts it is obviously critical that the program shall be able to represent and reason with statements like the ones shown above, or with the following:

"Did you receive my telegram?"

which the buyer has wired to the seller. We shall make no attempt to describe the representation of this feature. It has no bearing on the kind of problem we are interested in.

3.4.2.5 Conclusion.

Gardner's system is thus a rule-based system for case-law. While diagnosing 'hard' cases it is not able to do anything with them. Her system pinpoints the exact issues owing to which the case is 'hard', by reaching a situation where competing rules may be applied. After spotting the issue or issues, a more advanced system could then consider rules for and against a decision on the issue.

However, Gardner's thesis deals with other problems too. The difficulty with an interface with ordinary language and the problems arising from the knowledge representation are vast: The program has to deal with representation of reported speech, indirect discourse and connection between sentences. The program has no natural language interface (and does not need one). However, in the area of contracts it is critical that the program should be able to represent and reason about statements like:

"Will you supply carload of salt at $2.40 per cwt?"

Gardner herself is aware of this problem and its relation to the particular domain of law she has chosen. However, she justifies her choice of legal area by stating that if everybody were to choose legal areas like McCarty, only expert systems for taxation would be written. We shall return to this problem in the chapter five, when we discuss the choice of legal area for **JURIX**. Gardner's approach to open texture and 'easy' and 'hard' cases is of central importance to us. In chapter four we shall take up our discussion of these issues.

3.4.3 The HYPO System.

3.4.3.1   Introduction.

So far we have considered only rule-based systems.We shall now consider a case-based reasoning system: HYPO. It is developed by Edwina L. Rissland together with Kevin D. Ashley.

3.4.3.2 HYPO   Overview.

The HYPO system was developed by Rissland and Ashley for legal planning and analysis based on case-law. The system and various aspects of it have been described in a series of papers: [Rissland87] , [Ashley87a], [Ashley87b] and [Ashley88]. [Ashley89] deals with a formalization of the weighing process of HYPO. The entire work is described in detail in Ashley's book: [Ashley90], which essentially his Ph.D. thesis. The system operates in the area of trade secret law.

In this area of law plaintiff and defendant are often two corporations producing competing products. Information about the trade secrets of one corporation will sometimes be obtained by the other corporations in an illegal manner. For example, by theft or industrial espionage or through a former employee of the plaintiff corporation. A typical way for the plaintiff to argue his case is to show that the purported secret enabled the defendant to gain an unfair competitive advantage.

HYPO works in the following way. The user inputs a fact situation which is analyzed by the system. Next the system retrieves relevant cases from a case-base and 'positions' the retrieved cases with respect to the case at hand. Finally it selects important 'most-on-point' cases, suggests interesting hypothetical, related cases, proposes a skeleton of an argument and justifies the argument with case-citations.

As we shall see below, this system raises many important points concerning 'easy' and 'hard' cases. We shall first consider the architecture of the system in the next section. Next we shall see how it is actually applied. A comparison with other systems will be undertaken in chapter four.

3.4.3.3 Knowledge Representation.

The legal knowledge-base of the system consists of three parts:

(1) Factual Predicates.
This is a list of 31 predicates relevant to the area of law, called the factual predicates. Examples are ([Ashley90], appendix D):
i) 'Plaintiff makes a Product', which can attain the values: Nil, Product, Negative.
ii) 'Defendant saved Product Development Expense Relative to Plaintiff', which can attain the values: Nil, Product: List of development times and expenses, Negative.
For each new case to be analyzed the basic input is a list of the factual predicates satisfied by the case.

(2) CASE-KNOWLEDGE-BASE (CKB).
This is a set of 33 known (real and hypothetical) cases in the particular area of law which has been chosen - trade secrets law ([Ashley90], appendix E). Each case is represented as a hierarchical set of frames whose slots are important facets of the case, e.g. plaintiff, defendant, secret knowledge, employer/employee data.

(3) Library of DIMENSIONS.
A dimension is defined as a cluster of factual predicates having legal relevance for a particular claim, which are prerequisite for dealing with a claim and which contribute to weaknesses and strengths of a claim. Examples of the 13 dimensions of the system are: Aggreed-not-to-disclose, Competitive-advantage, Brought-tools ([Ashley90], appendix F). Dimensions are *not* necessary and sufficient conditions for a claim but rather fact-oriented

conditions for arguing that one case is stronger or weaker than another and should be decided accordingly. For each dimension there is at least one real legal case where the court decided the case because, or in spite of the features associated with the dimension. Thus the dimensions are *indices* to the cases in the sense of section 1.7.

The dimensions are the implementations of 'factors'. This central concept is described as follows:

"In HYPO, the legal concepts of relevant similarities and differences, most relevant cases, distinguishing and counterexamples are defined in terms of factors. Factors are a kind of expert knowledge of the commonly observed collections of facts that tend to strengthen or weaken a plaintiff's argument in favor of a legal claim." ([Ashley90], p.26).

A dimension is represented as a frame-like knowledge-structure. It has the following facets:

(1) Prerequisites, which are the factual predicates which must be satisfied for the dimension to apply.
(2) Focal-slots, which are related to the most important factual predicates.
(3) Ranges, which give numerical or binary symbolic values of concepts represented by the focal-slots.

Thus the dimension 'Secrets-disclosed-outsiders' has the focal-slot 'Number of Disclosures' and its corresponding range may contain the number of times secrets were actually disclosed. According to the value of a focal-slot a given dimension may be considered to have more or less *strength*.

3.4.3.4 Program Execution.

The user inputs what is called the current fact situation (cfs). This consists of a list of satisfied factual predicates representing the new case. HYPO then begins its legal analysis. It runs through the library of dimensions and produces a record (the D-list) of all dimensions which apply to the input data or which nearly apply. A dimension nearly applies, if the fact situation of the case at hand contains all the information needed to tell if the dimension applies except the information about magnitude that determines where the case should be situated along the dimension, i.e. the strength of the dimension is unknown. Such a dimension is called a 'near-miss' dimension. The system next retrieves cases from the CKB which are relevant, i.e. they have sets of dimensions that are subsets of the D-list of the case at hand. These are the matching cases.

The matching cases are ordered in what Rissland and Ashley call the claim lattice. This is a tree-like structure with the current case as root, and successor nodes ordered according to set-inclusion of their dimension-sets. The closer a case without near-miss dimensions is to the root, the more 'on point' it is supposed to be. Particularly it may be possible to chose 'most-on-point' cases for the plaintiff and 'most-on-point' cases for the defendant.

This ordering scheme of the retrieved cases captures a sense of closeness of cases from the CKB to the case at hand: All the retrieved cases are relevant to the current case as they share some legally important strengths and weaknesses with the given case. The claim lattice may now be used to select cases on which to rely, and to distinguish. It may also be used to generate legally interesting hypotheticals by changing the fact-situations. The system may be now used to compare the retrieved cases with the given case and among themselves. It creates a 3-ply argument consisting of (1) a point for one side, (2) response on behalf of the other side, and (3) rebuttal for the first side. It is done by weighing the dimensions according to specified rules in several steps, which we shall now explain.

3.4.3.5   Weighing   Schemes.

(1) The system first selects those dimensions for which there is at least one most-on-point case (mop-case). If all the mop cases were won by the same side, the selected dimensions are treated as indicating a similar decision for the given case.

(2) If there are mop-cases favouring the plaintiff and mop-cases favouring the defendant the system will attempt to discredit one set of mop-cases. This can be done by showing that these mop-cases are *distinguished*.

The system does this by finding dimensions present in the given case but not in the set of mop-cases to be distinguished. It can also do this by finding dimensions present in the set of mop-cases to be distinguished but not in the other set of mop-cases nor in the given case.

If no such distinguishing dimensions are present, the decisions in one set of mop-cases may be still be distinguished by considering the strength of certain dimensions. The system will attempt to show that the strength of some dimensions in the given case is less than the strength of these dimensions in one set of mop-cases. This set will therefore be the set to be distinguished. The 'strengths' of the dimensions are the values of the focal-slots stored in the ranges of the dimensions, as explained above.

(3) The final step is used to criticize and test the results of the first two steps. The system uses three methods based on the application of counter-examples.

Method One: Find a case with the same dimensions as the case in hand and the selected mop-cases, but more extreme with respect to slot-value strengths. Assume that it has a different outcome than the mop-cases selected. As we explained above (in (2)) this sometimes means that the case should be distinguished. However, if there are reasons to believe this is not so, it may indicate that the selected dimensions perhaps not are so important.

Method Two: The system may retrieve a case which contains not only the dimensions of the selected set of mop-cases, but also additional dimensions, whose values in the case at hand are unknown. This may be because they are non-existent or because the user did not tell HYPO about them, as he did not know of their relevance. If the decision of this case is different from the decision in one of the set of mop-cases, it may be used to discredit this set in the following way. If, by querying the user, the system will establish the truth of these additional dimensions the retrieved case would become a 'super-mop-case' discrediting the previously selected mop-cases as it has a different decision. If these dimensions are not true, the case may still be considered as a related hypothetical weakening the argumentation for following the selected set of mop-cases.

Method Three: The system will attempt to vary the strengths of dimensions from the selected mop-cases. Sometimes this will create a real case, a possibility we have already dealt with in (2) and above in Method Two. Sometimes the case obtained is a hypothetical case.

3.4.4 Hybrid Systems.

3.4.4.1 CABARET Overview.

The CABARET (CAse BAsed REasoning Tool) system developed by Rissland and Skalak represents a hybrid approach to legal reasoning. It combines case-based reasoning with rule-based reasoning in a domain-independent manner ([Rissland89], [Rissland89a]). In order to determine the meaning of a legal rule one must often apply both rules and past cases. Thus the area of 'Statutory Interpretation' is appropriate for the application of such a system.

The system:

"uses heuristic control rules to interleave case-based and rule-based tasks to solve problems in complex domains where knowledge both in the form of cases and in the form of rules is brought to bear." ([Skalak91], p.9).

The control heuristics are based on a theory of argument strategies and moves which may be applied in a domain where rules and previous cases are used to determine the interpretation of a given rule ([Skalak91]).

3.4.4.2   GREBE.

GREBE stands for GeneratoR of Exemplar-Based Explanations ([Branting91]). It is a hybrid system developed by Branting as part of his Ph.D. thesis ([Branting90]) in the area of Worker's Compensation Law (Texas).

When given a new case the system can reason about it using two methods of explanation (see [Branting89], p.104).

1) Generalisation-Based Explanation.

This is a rule-based method which attempts to explain a certain conclusion using a general domain rule. These rules are legal rules including both statutory rules, what Branting calls common law rules - presumably what we have previously defined as case law-statements (see 2.2.2) - and two kinds of common-sense rules.

The following are examples of the different kinds of rules taken from [Branting91], p.150:

Statutory law rule: "An employer is liable to his employee for worker's compensation if the injury is *sustained in the course of employment*" (Tex. Civ. St. Act 8309, par. 1).

Common law rule (first kind): "A passenger in a business carpool is in the course of employment whenever the driver is in the course of his employment, provided they have the same employer" (Janak v. Texas Employer's Ins. Co. 381 S.W. 2d 176 (1964)).

Common-sense rule: "If an activity is a duty of employment, then each necessary step of that activity is a duty of employment as well".

Common-sense rule (semantic kind): "A passenger is a kind of traveler. A traveler is a kind of agent".

There are altogether 57 legal and non-semantic common-sense rules and 132 semantic rules.

2) Exemplar-Based Explanation.

This method assumes that:

"...the similarity between a new case and the relevant aspects of a precedent justifies attributing the same conclusion to the new case as applied to the precedent" ([Branting89], p.105).

It has a case-base of 16 published legal precedents dealing with injuries sustained while a worker is travelling. It also contains 4 paradigm cases representing stereotypical situations ([Branting91], p.150).

An important feature of the case-based reasoner is its ability to reason with *portions of precedents*. We shall return to this feature in chapter four.

Another hybrid system is IKBALS II, developed by Vossos et al. (see [Vossos91]).

3.5 Two Proposed Approaches.

3.5.1 The Theory of Prototypes plus Deformations.

3.5.1.1 Introduction.

Parallel to the development of expert systems for case-law as exemplified by the systems described in the previous sections, the TAXMAN projects were running at Rutgers University, managed by L. Thorne McCarty. In section 3.2.3 we have described the TAXMAN I project. The continuation of this project is the still ongoing TAXMAN II project, which so far is of a more theoretical nature. The project has two strands. The first strand deals with a computational model of deontic logic ([McCarty83], [McCarty86]), a topic which we have described in section 3.3.3. The second strand deals with a computational theory of legal reasoning, which is of great interest for us. It uses extensions to the framework of *logical templates* developed in TAXMAN I, which are also represented in the AIMDS language (see [Sridharan78]). In this section we shall describe a theory of open texture proposed by McCarty ([McCarty82]), which is also part of the TAXMAN II project.

In order to present McCarty's theory, we shall first introduce a concept expressing the open texture of the law, central to the TAXMAN II project. It appears in the United States Tax Code after the Sixteenth Amendment was passed in 1913. Many problems arose over the definition of the concept "taxable income", which had no precise definition in the Act of 1913 in connection with the distribution of corporate earnings.

We shall here briefly mention a series of Supreme Court decisions concerning corporate dividends which attempted to deal with the problems that arose.

3.5.1.2 "Taxable Income".

The cases begin with Lynch v. Hornby: 247 U.S. 339 (1918). In this case Hornby received a cash dividend from the corporation in which he held stock. The U.S. Supreme Court held that a cash dividend is income and therefore taxable.

A second case was Peabody v. Eisner: 247 U.S. 347 (1918). Peabody held stock in a certain corporation. This corporation held stock in another corporation. It was decided to distribute the stock from this other corporation as a dividend, of which Peabody received his part. The Supreme Court decided that this stock dividend was also taxable income.

The third case to be considered is: Eisner v. Macomber: 252 U.S. 189 (1920). Macomber received as dividend stock in the corporation distributing the dividend. The Supreme Court held that this stock dividend was *not* to be considered as income and therefore *not* taxable.

The case is considered a landmark case to this day, as the judge delivering the majority decision (Pitney) attempted to define the concept of income. Since the argumentation and reasoning by the judges in this case is also of exceptional quality in both style and form, McCarty has chosen this case for exemplifying his theory.

3.5.1.3   Prototypes plus Deformations.

Prototype plus Deformation Theory attempts to present a model for reasoning within open texture. We shall follow [McCarty82] closely in presenting this theory. As an illustration he uses the concept of taxable income in the corporate domain, described above.

According to McCarty a legal concept expressing open texture will have three components:

(1) There is an *invariant* component. This component is optional.

(2) There is a set of *exemplars*, each of which matches some but not all of the instances of the concept.

(3) There is a set of transformations which express the *relationships* between the exemplars, i.e. which state that one exemplar can be mapped into another exemplar in a certain way.

McCarty suggests that it is often possible to delete some exemplars from the representation of the concept and to use the transformations to represent implicitly the missing elements. In some cases we may be able to do even better than this: it may be possible to represent the entire space by a single exemplar - a *prototype* - and a sequence of transformations - or *deformations* - of the prototype.

Schematically:

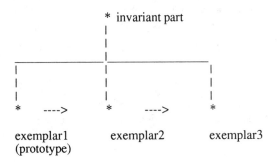

In [McCarty82b] a formal description of these concepts are given, using abstract definitions and concepts from AIMDS. However, the implementation is not complete. In McCarty's own words:

"The present theory is therefore only a "hand simulation": it poses computational problems at critical points (e.g., "generate a data structure with the following characteristics...") and then, without actually performing the computation, it exhibits the data structures..." ([McCarty82b], p.329.

We shall therefore give a very brief overview of the formal definitions using examples from the tax domain. Afterwards we shall describe the application of the theory to the case of Eisner v. Macomber, 252 U.S. 189 (1920) mentioned above.

The first concept we shall define is a so called DDN (data description). This is a data-structure describing a concept like "ownership by an actor of a share in a security which is issued by a corporation" ([McCarty82b], p.332). Another example of a DDN would be a structure describing the "transfer of cash from a corporation to its stockholders". The DDN may be considered as a generalization of the concept of a *logical template* described in 3.2.3.3. A *prototype* would be represented by a DDN.

The second central concept is the MAP structure. It is a data structure containing several parts. It contains:

(1) a DDN to be mapped,
(2) a DDN which is the image of the mapping,
(3) an invariant part, which is common to both source-DDN and its image, and
(4) a transformational part which may itself be a MAP structure. The *transformations* (*deformations*) of the theory are represented by MAP structures.

McCarty gives some examples of MAP structures which can be represented in the system. We shall bring two of his examples here:

(1) Let one DDN describe the transfer of cash from a corporation to its stockholders. The other DDN describes transfer of shares issued by another corporation from the owner company to its stockholders.

The 'transformation' is here the abstract correspondence between the two DDNs. The invariant part is the concept of 'transfer from corporation to stockholder of something'. This concept appears in both DDNs.

(2) Let one DDN describe some structure containing a continuous parameter, e.g. the proportional interest of a stockholder in his corporation. The other DDN would be the same structure after varying the parameter, i.e. after changing the proportional interest of the stockholder.

The transformational part is again the abstract correspondence between the two DDNs, and there is no invariant part.

McCarty now proposes to use combinations of several kinds of mappings to represent the process of legal argument. He suggest that legal concepts should be represented in the TAXMAN II formalism. The legal argument would then require the constructions of particular MAPs; each side would attempt to construct mappings in order to classify the case at hand with respect to other cases and hypotheticals. Each party would attempt to show that the mappings of other side are inconsistent or less coherent than his own.

In order to illustrate the applications of McCarty's theory, we shall consider the case of Eisner v. Macomber, 252 U.S. 189 (1920), mentioned above, and describe the legal argument according to McCarty's model.

The facts of the case were as follows: The Standard Oil Company had stock outstanding amounting to $50 Million out of an authorized capital of $100 Million. The company also had a large profit amounting to $25 Million. This profit was transferred from the surplus account to the capital stock account, and each stockholder was issued with a stock-dividend of 50%. Mrs. Macomber, being the owner of 2,200 shares of the old stock, received certificates for an additional 1,100 shares. The legal question was, whether this stock-dividend was taxable as income or not. The majority opinion, delivered by Justice Pitney, found the case to be non-taxable.

Among the arguments given by Pitney were the following two observations:

(1) The stock-dividend does not alter the pre-existing proportionate interest of any stockholder. If a stockholder had, say, 20% of the stock before the dividend he will *still* have 20% of the stock after the dividend. As the proportionate interest of a stockholder in a corporation determines his voting rights, it follows that the stock-dividend has not changed these voting rights.

(2) The aggregate assets of the corporation are not affected. As Pitney puts it: "The corporation is no poorer and the stockholder is no richer than they were before". The dividend really takes nothing from the the property of the company and adds nothing to the interests of the shareholders.

The above observations are used in connection with a hypothetical case of enrichment through increase in value of the capital (from fluctuations in the stockmarket). We shall call this case the 'unrealized appreciation case'. In such a case all agree that there is *no taxable income*. The question is now how to connect the above arguments with this hypothetical case.

We shall prefer not to use the MAP formalism from McCarty's Prototype plus Deformation model for this and the following examples, as its AIMDS representation is very extensive. Instead, we shall introduce a scheme we have found useful to summarize and represent arguments in a semi-formal way. Pitney's argument will look as follows:

Concept:	Non-taxable Income.
Prototype:	Unrealized Appreciation Case.
Deformation-Invariant:	(1) Constant Stock-Ratio. (2) Unchanged Corporate Assets.

This should interpreted as follows: Start out with the (hypothetical) Unrealized Appreciation Case. This is the prototype. Transform this into the Macomber case using the fact that in both cases there is (1) A constant stock-ratio and (2) unchanged corporative assets. (1) and (2) form the so-called *invariant* of the mapping. As the first, hypothetical case is not taxable neither is the second, real case.

The argumentation by Pitney represented the majority, but others argued differently. A minority opinion delivered by Justice Brandeis, considers some hypothetical cases.

Case One:

First a cash dividend and then sale of the corporation's own stock (bought up for this purpose, or newly issued) to the dividend receiver. All agree that this case is taxable.

Brandeis' argument may be represented as follows in our scheme for the Prototype plus Deformation model:

Concept:	Taxable Income.
Prototype:	Cash Distribution + Stock Purchase.
Deformation-Invariant:	Identical End Result as in Eisner v. Macomber: (1) Unchanged Stock-Ratio. (2) Unchanged Corporate Assets.

Case Two:

Another argument by Justice Brandeis considers a *sequence* of hypothetical cases: First a case where the question is the tax-liability of a stock-holder after the distribution of common stock, i.e. the Macomber case itself. Next a similar case where the distributed item is preferred stock, then a case concerning bonds, then long-term notes, then short-term notes and finally cash.

The claim is, that these cases are transformed (continuously) one into each other, and it would therefore be anomalous to classify Eisner v. Macomber as non-taxable, while all the other cases are agreed to be taxable.

Thus Brandeis' argument may be represented by another mapping. In our scheme for the model it looks as follows:

Concept: Taxable Income.

Prototype: Cash Distribution.

Deformation-   Transfer of Property from the
Invariant: Corporation to the Shareholder.

The prototype is here the case where cash is distributed. This is taxable income in the opinion of everybody. This case is now deformed into a case where the distributed item is short-term notes. The (invariant) property of both cases is that there is a transfer of property from the corporation to the shareholder. Here the income is also taxable. This case is now deformed into a case where the distributed item is long-term notes. Again there is the same invariant of the deformation. Finally one ends up with the Macomber-case, i.e. distribution of common stock. As in all cases we have had the same invariant, and as in all cases but the last the income was taxable, according to Brandeis it should also be so in the last, Macomber-case.

This brings us to a central question: Why is Pitney's model preferable to Brandeis' one?

McCarty does not give a full answer to this. Let us quote directly from [McCarty82]:

"Each party would then be searching through the description spaces to locate, or construct, those transformations which seem to impose the greatest degree of coherence on the set of exemplars".

3.5.1.4   Conclusion.

Our main reason for examining McCarty's theory of Prototypes plus Deformations is of course because it is the only piece of research directly addressing open texture. According to McCarty:

"The analysis of Eisner v. Macomber has been reduced to a series of computational problems: the representation of stocks and bonds, the specification of the syntax of the MAPs, the search through the space of DDN expressions. Once these problems are solved, the theory of Eisner v. Macomber will be fully computational, even implementable." ([McCarty82b], p.354).

The theory has been partially implemented in [Nagel87]. Unfortunately a full implementation has not yet been carried out. However, theoretical work related to the Prototype and Deformation Model is still going on and has been discussed in [McCarty91], which we shall briefly review.

First of all, McCarty has developed a new knowledge representation language: LLD - Language for Legal Discourse (see [McCarty89a]), which is based on intuitionistic rather than classical logic. The language has facilities for representing states, events, actions, permissions, obligations, etc., and there is a close correspondence between its surface syntax and its deep semantics ([McCarty91], p.187).

The problem presently being researched may be summarized as follows:

"What determines the choice of a prototype? What are the criteria for constructing transformations? It was clear that the set of transformations had to be tightly constrained, or else anything could be 'transformed' into anything. But what was the source of these constraints?" ([McCarty91], p.186).

McCarty's conjecture is that conceptual coherence (see above, section 3.5.1.3) can be explained, at least partially, by an analysis of the computational complexity of the inferences needed to be made in a language with the features of LLD. For further details see [McCarty89] , [McCarty91a] and [McCarty91b].

3.5.2 Bench-Capon and Sergot's Rule-Based Approach.

3.5.2.1 Introduction.

In chapter two we discussed the jurisprudential approaches and viewpoints concerning cases and the general rules they may embody. Gardner in her book [Gardner87] considers the use of examples and discards this possibility in favour of using rules (which she calls patterns). [Bench88] acknowledges the necessity of considering the cases themselves. The paper, however, proceeds to propose a use of general rules that may be of use also for 'hard' cases. We shall now consider this idea as discussed in the same paper.

3.5.2.2 The Rule-Based Approach.

Bench-Capon and Sergot suggest a legal system which assumes the existence of a data-base of cases (examples). The system does not reason directly from the *examples*, but reasons instead with *general rules* that these examples are able to generate. The builder of the system would formulate these tentative rules every time a new example is stored in the database. Examples are stored in the system, but only for the purpose of explaining and justifying the validity of the general rules. One example may generate several general rules, which may combine with others, and produce conflicting arguments.

As the authors point out, these rules extracted from examples are of dubious judicial status. Some of them are law-statements, law-specializations or law-generalizations (see chapter two for a definition of these concepts). But some rules should be generated just for the purpose of covering possible aspects of the open textured concept we are relating to. In fact, the more rules the better. In this way we ensure that the open textured concept will be covered entirely, and that the system will retrieve all examples that may be relevant to a given case involving the specific open textured concept.

We can never guarantee that these rules accurately express the facts of a particular decision, and we can never predict what feature of the given case will turn out to be relevant. For that reason we shall need several rules which apply, arguing for and against a conclusion, before we can reach any considered decision. This will also reduce the influence of a rule which is actually wrong. More importantly, there are bound to be cases where natural abstraction will contradict existing rules, which derive from other examples. Only in this way can one be sure, that the rules in the system do cover the concept completely.

By presenting and weighing the rules and the arguments, such a system could then be an aid to the user in dealing with a new case involving the same open textured concept.

3.5.2.3   Summary.

We recall Hart's characterization of open texture as creating a core of certainty where a given rule was valid, and a penumbra of doubt, where there would be reasons both for asserting and for denying the validity of the rule. [Bench88] proposes a method for dealing with these two abstract concepts. When given a specific case we shall attempt to extract as many general and possibly *conflicting* rules from it as we can. For a case in the core this may not be necessary, but if those rules cover the penumbra completely it will be possible to use them to reason about a case in the penumbra.

The authors of [Bench88] do not indicate how these rules should be constructed. Neither do they discuss how the rules should be weighted.

We have already mentioned that one of our reasons for undertaking the AXEMAN project was to gain sufficient familiarity with the area of law represented in McCarty's TAXMAN projects. We considered trying to apply the ideas of Bench-Capon and Sergot in that area of law. There are good reasons why this area of law may be inappropriate. We shall return to this in the next chapter.

Instead, we decided to consider quasi-legal domains. Chapter six describes our system, Meta, which is a shell based on the ideas of [Bench88] and implemented in a certain quasi-legal area.

3.6   Conclusion.

In this chapter we have given a broad overview of some of the related work done so far in the field of legal computer systems. We have described many methods of approaches, some of them obviously of great interest for the kind of academic system we are discussing, some of them of relevance only to experiential systems. However, the insight gained by understanding why a certain method applies only to an experiential system and not to an academic one is beneficial, for it often relates to the nature of the concept of open texture. In the next chapter we shall return to this point.

We have also described some important case-law systems. We have attempted in each case to describe the knowledge representation scheme and the knowledge utilization. It has been our aim to state the facts, leaving a comparison and general evaluation to the next chapter.

Finally we have described two proposed approaches to open texture of a more theoretical nature. Also their relation to the existing systems will be considered below.

4

Discussion of Previous Work

> The first thing to do, let's kill all the
> lawyers.
> (2 Henry VI, 4, 2)

4.1 Introduction.

4.1.1 General.

In the previous chapter we have surveyed various legal computer systems and their capabilities for either simulating legal reasoning or supporting it. We shall now attempt to develop a classification scheme for such systems, and review the systems along a path, so to speak, orthogonal to the one from chapter three, where we just considered the systems one by one.

Such a classification activity is usually considered an academic enterprise with merits of its own. We shall attempt it for an additional reason: It will provide us with an appropriate framework for discussing the existing systems besides the rule-based vs. case-based differentiation already defined and applied. As a matter of fact we shall consider severalseveral classifications and observe the various systems according to each of them. In a knowledge-based system it seems quite natural to search for such classifications with respect to the knowledge represented and utilized by the system.

Furthermore, in light of the jurisprudential preliminaries, previous work and our own ideas our aim is to discuss what can actually be *done* in the area of legal computer systems for case-law. Perhaps there are other computational devices (e.g. work on analogy) which can be brought to bear besides the techniques used by previous workers in the field. In the next two chapters we shall want to use this discussion and critique for design of our own case-law systems.

4.1.2 Kinds of Knowledge.

Concerning the various kinds of knowledge needed and utilized in a legal computer system, one can ask the following four questions (see [Winston84], p. 41):

(1) What kind of knowledge is involved?
(2) How should the knowledge be represented?
(3) How much knowledge is required?
(4) What exactly is the knowledge needed?

To those four questions we may add a fifth:

(5) How should the knowledge be utilized?

We can answer question one immediately. We shall distinguish between two kinds of knowledge to be represented and utilized in a legal system:

1. Common Sense Knowledge.
2. Legal Knowledge.

Below we shall deal separately with each of these kinds of knowledge.

Also question two may be considered here. As already pointed out in [Hafner87] the method of knowledge representation is not very important *in principle*. All the usual kinds of knowledge representation (semantic networks, logic programs etc.) provide the necessary structures. The choice may be one of efficiency, of convenience or of personal taste.

Thus it was straight forward to reconstruct TAXMAN I (which uses frames) in terms of rules (see section 3.2.3.4), and also Meldman's system, which uses semantic networks, was reconstructed in Prolog-logic.

The observation that the different knowledge representations are equivalent is sometimes formulated with respect to 'computational formalism' (see [Sergot91], p.10). It may perhaps be clearer to apply this latter concept to the use of different paradigms discussed in section 1.7 and related to question five raised above.

We shall give an example to illustrate this point. It is generally agreed that rules are of (at least some) importance in law, including case-law. Some may therefore be of the opinion that a legal computer system for case-law should use a rule-based knowledge representation. However, a rule-based *knowledge representation* does not necessarily imply a rule-based *computational approach.*

No comparative study has been made of the practical implications of the choice of knowledge representation. Some workers do not even mention their choice, which has to be deduced from related implicit information. Only Branting deals explicitly with this issue. He warns the system-builder that semantic networks:

"seem practical only in areas in which the range of factual variation is not too great and in which each precedent will be used frequently so that representation costs will be amortized over many users." ([Branting91], p.109).

Concerning question three and four: The legal knowledge sources are finite and definite, but could possibly be very extensive. In the area of nuisance there is no problem of collecting these sources and representing them even in a small computer. But the amount of cases needed in a computer system for, e.g., negligence is many times larger. As for common-sense knowledge, question three and four raise one of the central problems concerning legal computer systems, which we shall deal with separately in section 4.2.

This leaves only question five. We shall see below how other researchers have answered this question. Most of those answers are of course implicit in their systems and have not been formulated in any explicit manner until now.

4.2 Classification according to Common-Sense Knowledge.

4.2.1 Introduction.

By the name common sense knowledge we mean the unsaid additional facts and relations between facts that human beings understand and take for granted without being told explicitly. For example (see the description of Meldman's system in section 3.4.1.2): Fred Dobbs hits Benjie Hooray with his hockey stick. Human beings know about hockey games. The players are supposed to hit the puck, but it happens that one player will accidentally hit another player with his stick. If not told otherwise humans would probably assume that a hit was accidental, as part of the game. Computers do not know such things, but must be told explicitly to distinguish between accidental and intentional hits.

Furthermore, computers may sometimes have to be told about games in general. Why do people play games, why is it sometimes important to win but at other times a game is played without such considerations. What is the purpose of having a referee, substitution players and onlookers.

All the concepts we have just mentioned refer to just one example in Meldman's system, and we have certainly not attempted to be exhaustive in our covering of the knowledge related to this games-example. In order to build a practical system of the Meldman type in the area of assault and battery it will of course also be necessary to consider all the common-sense knowledge which relates to being afraid of threatening objects, to distinguish between objects which are threatening and others which are not, etc. It appears that there is no limit to the kind and amount of knowledge that humans usually take for granted.

It may be argued that the area chosen by Meldman needs an especially large amount of common-sense knowledge. We shall return to this point below and compare various areas of law used for legal systems and the amounts of background knowledge needed in these domains.

4.2.2 Facts-Driven vs. Concept-Driven Systems.

Consider again the nuisance case described in the introduction: Mr. White complains about Mr. Black's children playing football and hitting the ball over the wall into his garden. A facts-driven system would begin its execution by obtaining knowledge of who the plaintiff and defendant are, under what circumstances they live, what exactly happened, how many times, etc. These are the *facts* of the case. The aim of the system would be to establish (among other things) whether the alleged nuisance activity was reasonable or not. In order to do that it would need common-sense knowledge about football games, about windows being fragile, etc. In another case the process of establishing whether an activity was reasonable the system would need common-sense knowledge about all kinds of noises, or all kinds of water damages, etc. If this knowledge were present in the system, one could then input the *basic facts* of each new case and the system would attempt to analyze these facts and support reasoning about their legal significance.

Thus the basic idea of a facts-driven system is that the system would be able to input facts, choose among those facts the relevant ones and use its common-sense knowledge together with the facts to carry out the purpose for which it was built.

The other kind of system we intend to consider will be called a *concept-driven* system. In the White vs. Black case such a system would carry out its processing by establishing whether the concepts involved in proving nuisance (among them of course the concept of a reasonable activity) were true or false. It would support the user in deciding whether an activity was reasonable by considering other legal concepts, but it would not need the *basic facts* of the case for this process. How this may be possible and what the advantages of such an approach may be will be left for chapter five. This will be part of the design considerations for the **JURIX** system.

In chapter two, section 2.2.2 we mentioned a possible classification of legal reasoning. According to Susskind one approach which he denotes the 'bottom up' approach classifies the facts of a case in general terms and then subsumes that classification within the terms of one or more legal rules. This approach corresponds to a facts-driven system. The other approach, called the 'top down' approach by Susskind, starts with rules. They are broken down into derivations and then applied. This will correspond to a concept-driven system.

There are two possibilities for a facts-driven system:

(1) Type 1.

The system receives the basic facts-situation of a case, but cannot ask for additional information. It can proceed only on the basis of what it has been told initially. One possibility is now to assume that a system knows everything - which is totally unrealistic.

Alternatively we can let the system operate under the assumption that there is additional but unavailable information. Its answers will then be qualified or conditional, dependent upon relevant but unknown facts.

(2) Type 2.

The system has some facility to ask for (additional) information if required. As a matter of convenience, or to simulate real life, the system could collect some facts initially and ask for others as the need arising during the execution.

Consider now again the problem of how to cope with common-sense knowledge. It makes no difference *in principle* whether a facts-driven system is of the first or the second type. The amounts of common-sense knowledge needed to process a given case are the same in both types. A system of the first kind has a fixed knowledge-base to which we add the facts collected during the input process. This may or may not be sufficient for the declared purpose of the system. Our point is that the total knowledge is limited. As for the second type of system we observe, that querying-the-user does not extend the knowledge-acquisition capability. In order to ask about the *truth* of a certain fact the system must have previous knowledge about the *existence* of such a fact in principle and its relation to other pieces of information. There is therefore no difference between the method which inputs all facts initially, or asks for part of the information during the processing stage.

4.2.3 Problems with Facts-driven Systems.

How to represent and include all necessary common-sense knowledge is a major problem of all A.I. systems, including legal systems. As we have observed, a facts-driven system can contain only a fixed, initially given amount of common-sense knowledge.

Both the statutory-law systems we have considered, the systems by Meldman and Gardner are facts-driven. HYPO is facts-driven ([Ashley90], p.40), and also GREBE is facts-driven though this is not stated explicitly.

The TAXMAN I program inputs all facts initially (type 1) and the BNA program uses the query-the-user approach (type 2). Meldman's system begins with some initial facts and can ask the user for additional facts if necessary (type 2). The information published about Gardner's system and HYPO does not suffice to determine to which type they belong.

The problems that arise with facts-driven systems are not just of a technical nature, i.e., whether the pre-defined knowledge-base can be made sufficiently large or not. The nature of these problems is rather one of principle. In order to see that, consider the following example.

Assume that the plaintiff in an action for nuisance tells us that he is a 57 years old man with brown eyes who lives with his wife as a weekly tenant in a semi-detached house. He complains of a persistent noise originating from the motor in the refrigerator of his next-door neighbour.

The obviously relevant facts are: (1) He is a weekly tenant, (2) his premises adjoin the source of the noise. At first sight his age seems of no importance, and the colour of his eyes is almost certainly irrelevant. But how can we be sure of what are and what are not relevant facts in a case? Take, e.g., the age of the plaintiff. Assume that he were 87 years old and not 57. Perhaps he has become hypersensitive to noise with age. This is relevant because there are cases which suggest that his action in nuisance would not succeed. On the other hand, he may have become almost deaf with age and have an extremely strong case, if he nevertheless is bothered by the noise. In the majority of cases the age would not have any bearing at all.

We shall give another example of this kind of problem. The facts of Miller v. Jackson [1977] QB 966 are as follows: The plaintiffs bought a house the rear garden of which had a boundary with a cricket ground. They complained of incidents causing actual damage to their house and apprehension of personal injury which interfered with their enjoyment of their house and garden whenever cricket was being played.

The court held, that the nuisance was not the flight or hitting of the cricket-ball over the fence, but the *activity* of playing cricket. Furthermore, even the *threat* of injury was therefore considered enough for a nuisance action.

Here we observe that it is a problem on which activity to focus, as this activity may not be included among the facts supplied, but have to be inferred from them.

It is the responsibility of the human lawyer to elicit *all* the relevant facts from his client, to decide what is important among all the information supplied by the client and determine the relevant activities. This seems indeed to be an essential part of the legal process, perhaps even the central part of it. How could a computer system possibly accomplish this?

Were we to aim at building a system which would allow the user to input just any kind of fact that he judged relevant, the problem of understanding and organizing these facts would pose a very severe - perhaps insoluble - problem. Furthermore, one could never be sure the user would not go off in any odd direction and actually mislead the system. He may forget some facts and may not be aware of the importance of certain features if not prompted (like not mentioning the plaintiff's age in the above example).

It is instructive to consider what case-law systems of the existing types would do with examples of the above kind.

1.

A Meldman-type of system in the nuisance area could presumably have a precedent in its database where the age was found to be important and the plaintiff won accordingly. The system could then discover that the above case was similar to it and accept the same decision. However, it could never carry out (or support) any kind of reasoning related to the age where in a given case the problem is to discover whether the age is relevant or not. Neither could it conclude that at times when the age would be important it may still be possible to reach conflicting decisions in different cases (like illustrated above).

As for the second example, a Meldman-type system would be capable of dealing with facts only, and could not conclude anything relating to abstract concepts like the *activity* of cricket and *threats*.

One could of course ensure that the kind-hierarchy in a Meldman-like system would include information about these concepts. But there would be no end to the knowledge needed for a system with practical applicability.

2.

Gardner introduces special rules, called CSK-rules to deal with common sense knowledge. It is not clear whether the CSK rules in the system are appropriate only for the specific cases Gardner describes in her thesis or whether they are suitable for a wider domain.

Concerning the above example-cases, a Gardner-type system for nuisance would initially assume that the cases were 'hard' (as it always does). In the first case it would reach a decision only if it had common-sense rules about the age of persons and the relation of age to deafness and hypersensitivity. Moreover, it would need some kind of rules defining when age was *relevant* and when not. It is difficult to see how a knowledge-base could contain a sufficient amount of rules to resolve the problems of relevancy relating to just this single feature of age, not to mention all other possible features which humans instantly realize and know how to handle.

Concerning the second case, the problem is one of defining a common-sense knowledge-base which can pinpoint the *activity* of playing cricket as being important rather than the flight and hitting of a ball. Again, the amount of knowledge needed for a real, practical system would be prohibitive.

For Gardner's system the concept of common-sense knowledge is of extremely great importance because of her choice of legal domain. The notion of offer and acceptance can only be understood by introducing large amounts of common-sense and general knowledge into the program. A system that has to decide whether a certain answer is an acceptance must be able to distinguish between an answer sent as a letter and an answer sent as a telegram. It must know that there may be several differences between such answers, for example the time it would take for each of them to reach its destination.

Nevertheless, any given amount of common-sense knowledge could only suffice for a certain number of cases. One could always come up with a new case which the system would not know how to cope with.

3.

On input of the respective facts of the two example-cases discussed above to HYPO, it would retrieve related cases and organize them in the claim-lattice. Consider the first case. If a dimension called 'hypersensitive' is pre-defined using the factual predicate 'age' then precedents relating to hypersensitivity would be retrieved after input of the plaintiff's age. It would then be up to the human user to decide to which extent these cases were relevant or not. The system could possibly do that itself by applying its weighing algorithm. A similar argument can be made concerning deafness and age. The central point here is that the appropriate dimensions are pre-defined in the system and based on factual predicates. If it so happens that these factual predicates coincide with the ones that appear in the given case the system can function. If hypersensitivity in HYPO is not related to age, but possibly to other factual features, it cannot cope with the case. Thus the dimensions ought to be dependent on all possible facts in the case at hand *and in all other cases that may ever occur*. This is of course not possible.

Concerning the second case, the assumption must again be that a dimension called 'unreasonable activity' is pre-defined in the system, based on factual predicates like 'cricket-games' 'hitting of ball' etc. But an activity can be unreasonable not only because of cricket, but also because of football, handball, basketball etc. It can be 'unreasonable' because of thousands of other activities not related to ball-games at all. It is hard to see how the dimension 'unreasonable activity' could be defined using only a finite number of basic, factual predicates and yet cover a large part of the activities of everyday life.

With the exception of Meldman and Branting other researchers in case-law systems do not give any details relating to the problem of including sufficient common-sense knowledge in the descriptions of their systems. Meldman states exactly what knowledge is included in the kind-hierarchy. Branting considers two kinds of common-sense rules (see section 3.4.4.2) and gives their number. But other researchers do not supply this kind of information. It is therefore not possible to estimate the extent of *generality* of their systems. It is not known how large their knowledge-bases are, and whether the systems can deal with a large amount of cases each with an essentially different facts-background, or whether the systems have been implemented with general knowledge-bases appropriate for just a few pre-selected cases. These questions are of course important also for systems where the common-sense knowledge does not appear as a separate component of the system.

4.2.4 Summary.

In section 1.1 we pointed out that some areas of law are better suited for computer applications than others. A central reason for the unsuitability of a particular area of law is its dependence on common-sense knowledge.

For that reason battery and assault are perhaps not so appropriate - or perhaps not appropriate for the kind of system that Meldman built.

Furthermore, the area chosen by Meldman is unfortunately characterized by a great dependence on *establishing* facts rather than accepting certain facts. This feature seems to call for another type of system (an experiential system) instead of - or in addition to - the system Meldman has developed.

Other areas of law used for the development of case-law systems (contract law, trade-secrets law and torts) also exhibit great dependence on common-sense knowledge. But according to McCarty, Corporative Distributions and Reorganizations in U.S. Income Tax Law need far less common-sense knowledge than most other areas. Concerning the areas of contract law and law of torts he observes:

"It is inconceivable, as a practical matter, that a set of facts concerning the actions, beliefs, intentions and motivations of the parties in a contract or tort case could be represented in the TAXMAN I formalism with a detail rich enough to pose any interesting legal questions." ([McCarty80], p.29)

Meldman acknowledges the limitations of his approach: His generalization/analogy scheme is part of the common-sense knowledge of the system, yet, it can never be extensive enough for a practical system.

Gardner remarks that not everybody can be engaged in building legal systems in the tax domain, and that other areas should also be attempted, despite the problem of including the necessary common-sense knowledge.

Rissland and Ashley do not mention the problem of common-sense knowledge, though the concepts of a 'factual predicate' and 'current facts situation' (cfs) are central to their system.

As a final remark relating to common sense knowledge let us mention the existence of a principle (of questionable validity): If we choose a sufficiently small legal subdomain the corresponding common sense knowledge will also be very small[1] . This would mean that it would be easier to build computer systems in such a small area. There is no obvious or intuitive proof that this principle is true. Even if it is true, there is a distinct possibility that such an appropriately small legal subdomain will be so limited that it could give rise only to toy problems.

However, if we consider quasi-legal domains it may be possible to find areas where limited amounts of common-sense knowledge will suffice. If, e.g., we examine the `hard to heat' problem (first described in section 1.6.1) it should be possible to store *all* common-sense knowledge relevant for a computer system relating to that particular issue. As we shall see in chapter six, Meta uses this property to reason *exhaustively* about precedents.

Let us finally return to questions 3 and 4 from above: How much knowledge is required, and what exactly is that knowledge. What we have seen in this section is that there are no easy answers to these questions. In each area of law the answer will be different, and the capabilities of the system will be *strongly dependent* upon the amount of common-sense knowledge introduced. It appears that in most legal domains the vast amount of common-sense knowledge necessary makes a facts-driven system of limited application only. Future research in Artificial Intelligence may alleviate this problem (see, e.g., [Lenat90]).

---

[1] Mathematicians would call this an Epsilon-Delta principle.

4.3 Classification according to Legal Knowledge.

4.3.1 Inference Model.

One can generally classify computer systems according to the inference model and divide them into rule-based and non-rule-based systems. Systems using CBR are of course of the latter kind.

Concerning the concept of a rule-based system there is actually an entire spectrum of systems of this kind. At one end there are systems which are essentially theorem provers, at the other end of the spectrum are production systems. Sometimes only the latter type are called rule-based systems, while the former type are called deduction systems (see [Charniak85], p.437 and [Winston84], p. 177).

The system applied to the BNA and using APES is of course a deductive system. TAXMAN I, as we mentioned previously, is equivalent to a deductive system, and it is also possible to reconstruct Meldman's system in rule-based form. Gardner's system is essentially deductive. HYPO is case-based, CABARET and GREBE are hybrid systems, while TAXMAN II at present has abstract features only.

It is often considered a basic requirement that expert systems can explain and justify their conclusions. It makes the system more acceptable to human users by making its reasoning more clear and enable an evaluation of the reasoning process. This is also of importance when the system is used for educational purposes. Explanatory facilities also aid the developers in the debugging and modification of its knowledge-base.

It is easy to satisfy the explanatory requirement in a deductive rule-based system. Indeed, explanation and justification is an integral part of the BNA-system. Also Meldman shows how such explanations can be supplied by his system when requested. In the case of HYPO and CABARET the explanatory facilities of the systems form a central feature, as they generate appropriate legal argumentation. Also GREBE has 'memorandum generator'.

4.3.2 Complexity of Model.

The computer scientist P.E. Hart deals in a review article [Hart82] with the future of artificial intelligence. He distinguishes three classes of problems to be overcome in the area of expert systems. These problems may be characterized as three types of complexity to be dealt with: Conceptual complexity, computational complexity and developmental complexity. We shall consider these problems below as they relate to the area of legal case-law systems.

Problems of _computational complexity_ do not at present seem so important in the field of case-law systems as in some other fields, e.g. computer vision. The systems developed so far and mentioned in this book have required only moderate computational resources. They may, however, all be considered as prototypes. Their developers have intentionally chosen small and well-defined areas (or specific issues within an area) of law, and their knowledge-bases have been small.

Problems of _developmental complexity_ arise, for example, in the design and implementation of legal knowledge-bases. Were one to build a commercial system the preparation of large knowledge-bases would require significant resources and perhaps need development of special knowledge-acquisition tools (see [McCarty84]). Such problems are being dealt with successfully in the area of legal document retrieval, which we considered in the introduction. In the area of case-law systems there has so far been no practical experience beyond the prototypal systems we have considered.

Besides the developmental complexity one must also consider the problem of updating existing knowledge-bases. This problem has been considered in [Bench91] and [Bench91a] which stress the importance of 'isomorphic knowledge representation', i.e., the extent to which the structure of the knowledge base to reflect the structure of the legal source domain.

Bratley et al. assert that it is easier to add new cases to a collection than to add new rules to a rule-base ([Bratley91], p.73-74). They observe that a change of the statutory law may require the entire rule-base to be rebuilt.

However, coping with change may also be difficult in the case-based approach. Not only the case-base must be updated but also the _indices_ used for retrieving cases and perhaps also the corresponding weights. Prototypical systems built so far have all less than 100 cases in their respective case-bases, so practical experience of significance has yet to be obtained.

We shall now discuss some issues related to _conceptual complexity_. This discussion is also related to Winston's questions presented in 4.1.2. The choice of a conceptual model determines partially both the amount of needed knowledge and what it should be (questions three and four).

In [Hart82] it is pointed out that no crisp definition or qualitative measure exists for this notion. A conceptual model of a particular legal area may be taken as a set of concepts and relations among concepts sufficient to describe legislation, legal reasoning, cases and decisions in this particular area of law.

In this connection one can distinguish between 'shallow' (or 'surface') systems and 'deep' systems. By a shallow system we shall usually mean that conclusions are drawn directly from observed facts that characterize a situation. A shallow system does not need a representation of such fundamental concepts as causality, intent or basic physical principles. A deep system corresponds more closely to the notion of reasoning from first principles (see [Chandra83] and [Klein87]). The conceptual model used in a shallow (deep) system will correspondingly be called a shallow (deep) model, simple or complex as it may be.

In [Steels89] it is suggested that a 'deep' system is closer to a model of the human expert and that such a system: "offers graceful performance degradation and capabilities for better explanations and improved knowledge acquisition methods". In other words, such a system is often thought to be more robust and maintainable.

MYCIN (see [Shortliffe76]) is often described as a shallow system, while CASNET (see [Weiss78]) is generally considered a deep system.

MYCIN works by backtracking on a set of production rules that link observation and conclusion, while CASNET attempts to model the causal relations among the detailed disease states of a family of diseases (glaucomas).

To give a second example: HARPY ([Lowerre80]) is a shallow system while HEARSAY II ([Reddy76]) is a deep system for speech understanding. HARPY compiles all knowledge of speech and language into a graph that is then searched to find a legal utterance, whereas HEARSAY II has explicit representation for knowledge at phonetic, syntactic, semantic and other levels.

As [Hart82] puts it:

"At the extremes a shallow system directly associates input states with actions, whereas a deep system makes deductions from a compact collection of fundamental principles."

One should not, however, confuse shallowness with lack of usefulness. If the experiential system is built using domain knowledge from a true expert - as, e.g., Capper for the Latent Damage System - it can have great practical applicability. Considering the state of the art this is probably not yet true of academic systems which are prototypes and in most cases cannot be expanded/improved to be of actual applicability.

Now, McCarty argues:

"... the most critical task in the development of an intelligent legal information system, either for document retrieval or for expert advice, is the construction of a conceptual model of the relevant legal domain." ([McCarty84])

From what follows it appears that McCarty actually argues for a *deep* conceptual model of the legal domain. Unfortunately he does not define exactly what he means by that. Instead, he just brings the TAXMAN formalism as an example of such a deep conceptual model (see quote from [McCarty82] in section 3.2.3.3). The models suggested by McCarty in [McCarty83] and [McCarty86] which are based on concepts of permission and obligation would also be considered 'deep' models.

In a later paper ([McCarty89a]) McCarty recognizes the puzzlement about the term `deep conceptual model' as expressed by other writers (see [Susskind87], p.149-155). He proceeds to give the following explanation of the basic idea:

"There are many common sense categories underlying the representation of a legal problem domain: space, time, mass, action, permission, obligation, causation, purpose, intention, knowledge, belief and so on. The idea is to select a small set of these common sense categories, the ones most appropriate for a particular legal application..." ([McCarty89a], p.180).

A deep model could be based on the deontic concepts of permission and obligations as mentioned before. It could also model the underlying domain in some 'deep' conceptual manner based on theories of criminology, sociology etc.

One may naturally inquire into the depth of the other existing legal systems. This can be done by comparing them to the shallow/deep models exhibited by MYCIN/CASENET and HARPY/HEARSAY II.

While the models used in Meldman's, Gardner's and the HYPO system are obviously not shallow, this is perhaps not so straightforward to see in the case of the BNA formalization project, which uses 'hyphenated predicates' like:

"was-found-abandoned-as-a-newborn-infant-in-the-UK'.

Indeed, McCarty, when discussing the CORPTAX program ([Hellawell80]), has called systems with such unstructured predicates for shallow systems (see [McCarty83a], p. 17-23). However, Sergot in [Sergot86] distinguishes between concepts that involve points of law and concepts which involve only points of fact. The hyphenated predicates are used only for the latter kind. This is related to features of the represented legislation and *not* because the domain model is shallow. To use another metaphor, hyphenated predicates do not necessarily indicate that the *granularity* of the system-representation is *coarse*.

Now the law itself is usually not formulated as rules in deontic logic or expressed with the help of such (deep) concepts, and many computer systems aim at representing the law. One may therefore distinguish three levels of 'conceptual depth'.

(1) The deepest level attained by system operating with Hohfeldian concepts. [Sergot91] suggests that a system using primitive ideas resembling Schank's conceptual dependency theory ([Schank74]) would also be (very) deep.

(2) The intermediate level attained by computer systems aiming at representing the law. This would be the level of all academic system mentioned so far.

(3) The shallow level exhibited by most experiential systems.

We may ask whether the choice of conceptual level is indeed of fundamental importance for legal systems. Peter Hart, speaking generally in the survey paper quoted above, believes that future accomplishments will mainly lie in deep systems.

Now Sergot remarks ([Sergot86], p.34) that the important thing to capture when building a model for a case-law system is not only the relationships, but also the constraints which obtain between the primitive concepts. However, the example that he gives: "Fathers are always Male", belongs properly to the domain of common-sense knowledge, while we are concerned with depth of the legal model.

Also Bench-Capon discusses the actual importance of deep models for legal computer systems in [Bench89]. He makes some very relevant observations:

(1) A strong argument in favor of deep models is the lack of a certain kind of explanatory capability in shallow systems. A legal system should not only arrive at the correct conclusions, but it should arrive at these conclusions in a convincing manner, i.e. based on the law. Rules elicited from a human legal expert do commonly not express the causal relationship with the law itself, even though these relationships may be underlaying the

human expertise. Deep models, on the other hand, could show these relationships in an explicit and hence convincing manner.

(2) There is yet another advantage to the explicit representation of the causal relationship of the expert knowledge and the law in a system based on a deep model: It is often easier to maintain such a system than a shallow system based exclusively on empirical associations. The initial knowledge acquisition for a deep system may possibly also be more convenient and easier than for a shallow system.

(3) The knowledge present in a shallow system (elicited from an expert) may be incomplete in the sense that it may be possible to find cases this knowledge simply does not relate to. The knowledge in a deep system would supposedly be able to cope with all cases.

These arguments also apply if one compares shallow systems to systems (of intermediate depth) based on a formalization of the law. Bench-Capon is mainly referring to formalizations of statutory law, but this seems also to be true of rules derived from precedents and representing case-law (case law-statements).

He observes that in rule-based systems developed by formalizing law-statements there is a more or less explicit correspondence of the rules to the law itself. In [Bench91] this is called an *isomorphic* knowledge representation. In such systems the explanatory facilities could therefore easily be based on the law itself. Also the maintenance of the system could be carried out with the same or perhaps even greater ease than in a deep system, as we have already mentioned above.

It may thus be argued that rule-based systems of intermediate depth, derived by formalization of the law can be of *major* use, as they have most of the advantages of deep systems. However, such systems could not deal with all cases. There are certain limitations to their use, as we explained in section 3.2.2, when we discussed the BNA-project. The application of systems based on rule-formalizations is appropriate for 'easy' cases (see 3.2.2.2), but owing to the need to consider open texture one must apply deep models in order to deal with 'hard' cases. As McCarty's TAXMAN project is specifically dealing with open texture, it is therefore no surprise that he argues for deep conceptual models. We shall return to the subject of shallow and deep systems in section 4.4.2.

4.3.3 Case Representation and Retrieval.

We have already seen several ways of representing cases in a legal system. We shall now assess the methods used in the various systems for representing, retrieving and applying previous cases.

I. Meldman's System.

Meldman represents a case by a single fixed rule (the ratio, a case law-statement). There are no conflicting rules.

As already explained he attempts to match the case at hand to one of the cases in his knowledge-base. If no such match is found the system cannot carry out any kind of reasonable analysis. A real case will of course be decided by a judge no matter whether a relevant precedent is found or not. Anyway, this approach is not very realistic. In practice there will often be several more or less *similar* cases, but none which has *exactly* the same features.

Even when a single similar case is found, Meldman's model is too simplistic (as he acknowledges himself). In order to apply case-law, Meldman's strategy is simply to adopt what seems to be the ratio decidendi of the matched case, stated explicitly as a rule. This ignores the fact, that there may be several rationes in one case and also obiter dicta, which could be relevant. Furthermore, as we have mentioned previously, the ratio is not always clear and precedents are used in many, sometimes strange ways (see, e.g. [Llewellyn60]).

As we mentioned before, in practice there will be more than one applicable case to retrieve and apply. This leads to what perhaps is the most serious defect of the system: The lack of reasoning with several relevant cases, that all are somehow similar to the given case, but may have different conclusions.

There is another weakness in the approach to legal analysis. Matching the case at hand with a similar precedent is only one aspect of legal analysis. It very often happens, that a lawyer selects a specific case not because it necessarily is analogous to the case at hand, but because it may be used to persuade the judge that the proposed rule of law actually does exist. There may actually not be a single fact common or similar in the two compared cases. However, this aspect of legal reasoning is completely absent from Meldman's system.

There are great limitations in Meldman's approach to generalization/analogy. Consider, e.g., a case in nuisance where the alleged activity is *intermittent*. The lawyer for the plaintiff would undoubtly try to bring many arguments and precedents similar to the case at hand in favour of his client. But there are also other approaches utilized by a lawyer. He may, for example want to show that the feature of intermittency is central to the case and should be taken into account by the judge. He may therefore choose to cite the case: Rapier v. London Tramways Co. [1893] 2 Ch. 588 in court. In this precedent the plaintiff complained of noise nuisance from horse stables belonging to London Tramways. Kekewich J. found for the plaintiff stating:

"An intermittent noise, particularly when it does not come at stated intervals is likely to be more disagreeable than if it were constant".

Now a modern case would probably not be related to noise made by horses but could deal with noise created, say, by machinery. A Meldman-like system could deal with such cases assuming an appropriate kind-hierarchy.

However, the case may not be concerned with a *noise* activity at all, but some other activity which occurs intermittently. The only reason the lawyer has for bringing this case is to argue that an intermittent activity is very irritating for the plaintiff. The judge is of course not bound to accept this argument, but a lawyer could very well decide to use it.

Consider for example the (football) case of White vs. Black. Mr. White's lawyer could decide to argue that if the children would play only between the hours of 2 p.m. and 4 p.m. the situation would be bearable for his clients. However, the fact that the activity is intermittent - they never know when the ball is going to fly over the wall - is what makes them suffer. He could then cite the above case, and any human would see the relevance immediately. However, an analogy system which would find the connection between intermittent noise and intermittent football games will have to be far more advanced than Meldman's system.

II. Gardner's System.

Gardner represent cases by rules called 'patterns'. There may be several patterns derived from one case, and several cases may define one pattern. Patterns may also be based on hypothetical cases.

Gardner gives some argumentation why the case knowledge should be abstracted and expressed by the patterns. Assume we represent each case by a collection of facts (and by its decision). Consider now a new case and assume we want to retrieve precedents relating to this case. Obviously not every case having certain facts in common with the case at hand should be retrieved. On the other hand, we can never know which facts precisely are important for the decision of the new case.

Gardner resolves the dilemma by applying *all possible* rules (patterns). As we have already explained in chapter three, if the rules do not conflict the case is 'easy'. If the rules conflict, but the conflict may be resolved by applying common-sense rules the case is also 'easy'. Gardner argues that in 'easy' cases we *do* know what the relevant facts are, and that this knowledge may equivalently be formulated by applying 'patterns' which are all true (in the logical sense).

Nevertheless, there are reasons against the approach used by Gardner. Suppose a lawyer or a judge considers two cases with opposite decisions which in his opinion both apply. This does not mean that he automatically gives them the *same* weight. After some consideration he may decide to give one case a more central position in his deliberation. Thus what may initially seem to be a hard case would resolve itself as an easy one. In Gardner's system opposing rules always lead to a hard case.

Among the functions of Gardner's CSK rules is one similar to the function of Meldman's kind-hierarchy, so one may inquire into the limitations of the system with relation to analogy. However, because of the rule-based approach a Gardner-type of system could cope with the intermittency example discussed above. It uses general patterns and may have a rule which in an oversimplified form could be:

nuisance **i f** intermittent activity

There are other issues that a system based exclusively on rules cannot deal with. When we discussed Meldman's system we explained that a lawyer sometimes will cite a case in order to show that a certain rule exists, even though the cited case and the case at hand have no (obvious) similarities. The cited case could even be from an entirely different area of law. It does not seem practical for a Gardner-type system to include all *possible* rules, especially from other areas, in the knowledge-base.

There may also be other reasons for using a case itself and not just a rule representing it. For example, one may want to use a case in legal reasoning for the *process* by which a decision is reached and not for the rule itself, as we shall now explain.

A lawyer may cite a previous case which has no similarity at all to the case at hand. Its decision or the rule that can be derived from it may not even be applicable to the given case. Nevertheless, the lawyer could argue that the *process* by which the judge arrived at the decision in the previous case should also be applied in his case, presumably yielding the decision he seeks. This kind of legal reasoning cannot be carried out in Gardner's system where only the relevant rules are considered. To be fair, it should be mentioned that at present there is no such capability in *any* system.

III. HYPO.

HYPO organises the set of known and hypothetical cases by their facts. The cases may then be retrieved according to the dimensions, i.e., clusters of facts which are found to be of importance in the legal reasoning of lawyers in the given domain.

There are several advantages which relate to the retrieval of cases according to dimensions.

(1) Matching according to facts may be computationally too complex except in special cases. The use of dimensions reduces this complexity.

(2) There may be considerable variability in the fact-content of cases which present the same claim. Again, the use of dimensions ensure that the retrieved cases are *legally* relevant.

The idea of dimensions capture an important aspect of legal reasoning: The importance of several facts combining to determine the truth-value of a certain legal concept. However, as Rissland and Ashley recognize, legal dimensions do not act independently, and a model based only on dimensions is inadequate. We shall now point out some features of legal reasoning which are not reflected in the use of dimensions.

HYPO retrieves 'most-on-point' cases (mop-cases), i.e. cases which are nearest the case at hand in the 'claims-lattice'. This means that a mop-case is one which has the *most* dimensions in common with the dimensions of the case at hand, i.e. the most coinciding facts which are of legal significance. This kind of retrieval undoubtly represents one approach used by lawyers in legal reasoning. As we just pointed out, there are other methods of using cases than the 'mop-case' method. A case with just *one* fact in common with the case at hand may sometimes be more convincing than a case with many such common dimensions. Even though it may seem somewhat far-fetched, one can imagine a (non-noise) activity being judged as nuisance because it is intermittent and because the judge decides to follow the above cited case concerning noise-nuisance. This kind of legal reasoning is not reflected in HYPO.

Capabilities of using cases in order to show that a certain rule is valid or in order to illustrate the applicability of a certain decision-process do not exist in HYPO.

[Mendelson89] discusses the suitability of the method of dimensions in other areas of law. He has applied the method to the law governing Government appeals in criminal cases. He distinguishes two problems with this approach.

(1) In some instances, the factual details proved crucial to a proper representation of the case, while the dimensions did not reflect this. The reason for this fact-sensitivity could be related to his choice of an area of criminal law.

(2) This particular area of law appears to be unsettled. The method of dimensions does not deal properly with the shifting emphasis of the court. We shall return to these observations while discussing the **JURIX** system in chapter six.

IV. GREBE.

This system is capable of connecting a meaningful portion of the facts to intermediate conclusions. Furthermore, it uses general rules when possible. Thus two of the criticisms of HYPO do not hold for this system.

V. Other Methods.

This is an appropriate place to reconsider the retrieval methods described in 3.3.4.2.2 (nearest neighbours) and 3.3.4.2.3 (citation vectors). Both methods use statistical techniques for retrieving one or more cases which are similar to the case at hand according to some predefined measure, relating to words or citations. Owing to such techniques the methods are of course appropriate for an experiential system. However, they have no place in an academic one. Depending on the choice of weights and similarity measure the methods may sometimes be good and sometimes bad: Given a new case one can never be sure the methods will retrieve *all* the relevant cases and *only* those cases.

These methods may be improvements upon the classical document retrieval techniques, but this is insufficient for an academic system. HYPO, on the other hand, retrieves *all* relevant cases it aims at retrieving according to the method of dimensions.

[Greenleaf87] defines the 'most persuasive' case: Using the 'nearest neighbour' method this is the case which together with the given case yields the greatest similarity measure. Using the terminology of HYPO this case could correspond to a special situation where there were exactly one mop-case. However, the 'most persuasive' case is chosen statistically and may therefore not be identical to the (unique) mop-case at all. It thus seems that even an experiential system would need additional techniques for case-retrieval besides the nearest neighbour method, or at least consider other 'similar' cases in addition to the 'most persuasive' one.

Finally we shall consider the conceptual retrieval method described in section 3.3.4.3. All the appropriate cases relevant to a given new case can here be retrieved. The question is how to look for these cases in an appropriate manner. The way to make such requests (as [Hafner87] proposes) is to use an issue/discrimination tree. The 'issues' Hafner is referring to are similar to the dimensions of HYPO (as she acknowledges) and, like the dimensions, carry links to the relevant cases.

4.3.4 Open Texture.

4.3.4.1 Existing Systems.

We shall now consider the issue of open texture and related concepts. In chapter two we raised a question as to the importance of the 'easy'/'hard' distinction. These concepts are very convenient when discussing cases or issues arising in cases. Instead of having to explain that in a given case there may be arguments for a certain decision and also arguments against it, and that a conflict has no obvious resolution, one may concisely put it that the case is 'hard'.

However, a computer system could retrieve cases and arguments for conflicting decisions also in the 'easy' case. It would then be (more or less) obvious to the professional user which cases and arguments to choose and which where only incidental on the case. Indeed, this is the approach of HYPO. Thus the 'easy'/'hard' distinction is not necessarily central in an *advisory* system.

There may be additional reasons for not giving too much importance to these concepts. It is widely accepted that most cases are 'easy'. So these are the ones that occur most of the time. On the other hand, *any* case can be turned into a 'hard' one by raising questions about the applicability of a particular rule, or rather of *any* rule. Again, if a system uses the approach of HYPO, the user could decide to which extent the case really is 'hard' or only is made to seem so by an energetic lawyer.

If a system does consider these concepts, it should, however, supply an answer to the two questions we formulated in section 1.6.1:

(1) When considering a concrete case, how do we know whether it belongs to the 'core of certainty' or to the 'penumbra'?

(2) If indeed a particular case belongs to the 'penumbra' what should the system do with it?

In chapter three we already considered the approach of the two statutory systems to open texture. In the case of the BNA system we explained that the formalization of the Act could be considered in three ways.

(1) The formalization yields a single, fixed interpretation of the law and thus ignores the open texture of the law.
(2) The formalization expresses the open texture, but an approach which forces the user to give only yes/no answers lacks a consideration of open texture.
(3) The system is applicable only for 'easy' cases. For only in the latter is it possible to overcome the open texture of the law.

Concerning the TAXMAN I system we also saw that the same three viewpoints are possible.

Meldman's treatment of open texture is identical to the similar approaches in the described statutory-law systems. This is not surprising. We have already described Meldman's model as a statutory-law system + analogy/generalization (in section 3.4.1.3). The law is described by a set of non-conflicting law-statements, and the facts of a given case are subsumed directly or by analogy/generalization within the set of law-statements. This subsumption is always clear-cut, i.e. open texture is either ignored, or alternatively as we saw, the cases the system can deal with must always be assumed to be 'easy'.

While the statutory-law programs and Meldman's system treat all cases as 'easy', Gardner's system has the capability of diagnosing a 'hard' case. However, it does not attempt any further processing of such a case.

We have already mentioned that HYPO does not directly address the problems of open texture, nor does it explicitly distinguish 'easy' from 'hard' cases. Rissland and Ashley therefore do not give explicit answers to these two questions. However, we may attempt to relate HYPO to the questions by considering the weighing process described in 3.4.3.5:

(1) If all the mop-cases retrieved and ordered in the claims lattice all point the same way (i.e. to the same decision) the case at hand seems to be 'easy'.

(2) If not, i.e. there are mop-cases in the claim lattice which point both ways (and one set of mop-cases cannot be distinguished or discredited), then the case is 'hard'.

Concerning the second question: If the case is 'hard' (indeed, also if it is 'easy') the system retrieves all relevant cases and organizes them in a manner convenient for the user who has to make a final decision concerning the case at hand.

What in our opinion seems to be the single most important idea in the HYPO system is the capability of giving some kind of legal structure to the prerequisite facts. But the dimensions also express the importance of the degree or *strength* of some attribute of the legal situation. The legal concepts are organized by the dimensions so that the most important ones can be analyzed and manipulated in a legally meaningful way, for instance, to strengthen or weaken a case. To illustrate this consider the dimension "Disclose-secrets'. It captures the knowledge that the *more* people who have been told about the secret, the *worse* off the teller is.

The concept of strength is implemented only for purely numerical features like the number of times secrets were disclosed, or for binary values (e.g., something/nothing). This ought possibly to be extended to the weighing of non-numerical but enumerative features.

By retrieving cases and attempting to weigh them HYPO confronts the problems of open texture. What seems most important, though the authors do not state that, is the inclusion not only of mop-cases but also of near-misses in the D-list, and hence the retrieval of cases which have *slightly* different fact-situations. The authors mention that this property of the claim-lattice is used to generate interesting hypotheticals.

However, it seems also correct to say that the retrieval of these cases is necessitated by and expresses the open texture of the legal situation at hand. When a case belongs to the 'penumbra' it means that it can be argued two ways. The reason for that is usually that one can retrieve cases, which are very similar to the case at hand with different decisions. The more related cases the better, for each one may illustrate another aspect of open texture. Presumably not all of these cases would be mop-cases, but some of them could be near-misses or near hypotheticals.

Branting explicitly mentions that his system is capable of 'term reformulation', i.e.: "the process of replacing an open-textured predicate with one or more predicates for which there are precedents that more closely match the new case" ([Branting91], p.153). His system does not directly address the distinction between 'easy' and 'hard' cases. As with HYPO this means that all cases are initially considered 'hard'.

4.3.4.2 Proposed Approaches.

We have seen that the existing systems either ignore the open texture of the law

(Meldman), diagnose 'hard' cases (Gardner) or behaves as if it assumes initially that all cases are 'hard' (HYPO). The latter system also includes a process of weighing the retrieved cases. However, this weighing process is not complete, but should be considered as advising and guiding the human user of the system. As we have mentioned before, there are also other aspects of legal reasoning not covered by the dimensions-approach.

The open texture of the law indicates that a certain process should take place in arguing for and against a decision. This process humans know how to carry out. Obviously the process should refer to the appropriate legal sources. Lawyers and judges do so, and computer systems can at least carry out a retrieval of the appropriate legal material. But it is not clear how the reasoning process should be carried out in a computer system.

McCarty's theory of Prototypes plus Deformations attempts to formalize this process. But it is not clear how a computer system should deform a given case to connect it to supporting as well as to contrary, existing cases and hypotheticals.

McCarty's theory speaks about joining two disparate cases through a series of incremental changes. However, the area he has chosen, taxation of corporate distributions and reorganizations, is characterized by the *discontinuities* of a series of historical decisions of the U.S. Supreme Court (see section 3.5.1 and also [Brody80]). If the space in McCarty's theory is too sparse in the tax-domain, one may possibly create hypotheticals to fill it out. Such hypotheticals would anyway be of importance in determining the appropriate exemplar for a deformation. Nevertheless, it is hard to see how exactly this process of deformation of cases and joining of the initial and final cases may be implemented.

We may compare this situation with the theory of Bench-Capon and Sergot. Their proposal seems to be more adaptable for implementation than McCarty's from a practical point of view, as it operates with rules. For example, hypotheticals may be created or cases changed by adding or taking rules away. An implementation of this theory, using methods of logic programming, should be feasible.

There is, however, a practical problem involved. There seem to be a great dependency on the area of law chosen for implementing the theory. In most areas of law the decision in a given case involve the weighing of arguments (equivalent to the rules mentioned above) relating to *several* (open textured) concepts. In order not to create a problem of too great complexity one should choose the legal area with care. It should have many cases all of them relating to just one concept (like, e.g. 'hard to heat'). It should be sufficiently 'dense' in the sense that it should be possible to create many (conflicting) rules all relating to one specific concept expressing the open texture. The domain of 'hard to heat' rules is perhaps a good example for this, though nobody has attempted an implementation yet. From a purely practical point of view, it may not be easy for a researcher to gain access to the relevant material in this area, i.e. the cases and their decisions. For that reason Meta has been implemented in an area where information was readily accessible.

One of our reasons for undertaking the AXEMAN project was to gain sufficient familiarity with the area of law represented in McCarty's TAXMAN projects. We considered trying to implement Bench-Capon and Sergot's ideas in that area of law. Unfortunately this is problematic, as McCarty's area is characterized by the behaviour of the open textured concept 'income'. We have already mentioned that the series of U.S. Supreme Court decisions relating to 'income' (see [McCarty82] and [Brody80]) seem to exhibit discontinuities and, on the face of it, do not supply sufficiently rich material for creating a large amount of rules as needed for the Bench-Capon and Sergot approach.

On the other hand, McCarty's theory of Prototypes and Deformations seems to be very general and less dependent on the selected legal domain. In its present, unimplemented form it can be used by humans as an aid in formalizing legal argumentation and understanding the reasoning by the court. The paper by Brody ([Brody80]) is a good example of this in the TAXMAN area. This paper discusses a series of cases in the area of corporate reorganizations and corporate distributions which followed the Macomber case. It succeeds in formulating the legal argumentation of the Supreme Court Justices using the theory of Prototypes and Deformations. However, it does not appear to be easy to carry out an implementation program of this theory whether in this area (corporate tax-law) or some other area of law.

4.4 Assessment according to System-Structure.

4.4.1 Introduction.

In the previous sections we have considered various classifications of computer systems for case-law. We have analyzed the existing systems accordingly and discussed the extremely difficult problems they have encountered.

In order to carry out some design considerations for future systems one must consider some additional issues:

(1) Which approach to choose: Academic or Experiential System.
(2) Who is the user of system: Judge or Lawyer.

In this section we shall deal with such engineering considerations, and draw some relevant conclusions. In the next part of the book we shall show how suggestions based on those conclusions have been implemented in the **JURIX** system.

4.4.2 Academic vs. Experiential System.

One may attempt to argue that the difference between an academic and an experiential system is only a matter of degree: The academic system focuses on the law itself, while the experiential system attempts to focus on what is *probably* the law.

Consider for example the method of extracting the 'most persuasive' case described in section 3.3.4.2.2. This method may not always work, as the weights and similarity measure may be all wrong for a given case. Nevertheless, the *objective* of the method is the same as one would want from an academic system: To retrieve a case which will supply a rule of law that may persuade a judge how to decide the case at hand.

There are, however, other aspects of experiential systems which are entirely foreign to the conception of an academic system. We shall illustrate this by reconsidering the (imaginary) case described in section 1.5, where Mr. White complained about the children of Mr. Black who played football in the neighbouring garden to his and his wife's discomfort.

Consider the following (apocryphal) continuation of the story (which we assume did not happen in the U.K.). Mr. White (or rather his wife) was most insistent on taking the matter to court, despite the fact that his lawyer advised against it. He had told Mr.White that the incidents were so insignificant and far between, that the law was undoubtly for Mr. Black. His only chance of winning would be if the case went to the court of Judge X, as it was well known that this judge disliked children immensely.

Now in the country where this story takes place, cases are allocated to the judges alphabetically, according to the surname of the plaintiff. The lawyer suggested to Mr. White that he change his name to Mr. Aardvark. (In that particular country this can be done for a small fee with immediate effect). After Mr. White did so, the case was indeed allocated to the court of Judge X.

The lawyer succeeded in having Mr. Black bring his children to court. After five minutes the judge sternly told the children to be quiet (though they were actually behaving properly). After another ten minutes the judge threw the children out of the court-room, and after an additional quarter of an hour he found for Mr. White (Aardvark).

Given the facts of the case the correct answer given by an academic system should be that Mr. Black, the defendant ought to win. An experiential system, however, having access to special knowledge about the personality of Judge X and about court-house procedure, could possibly come up with the approach successfully suggested by Mr. White's lawyer.

For a real-life illustration of this point see the reminiscences of Felix Frankfurter as described in [Phillips60], p.98-101.

It is possible to argue that experiential and academic systems form a continuum, with a purely experiential system based on the kind of knowledge just illustrated occupying one extreme. At some distance from that system one would find the LDS and the TAXADVISOR systems (see 1.4) and a little further on the system for finding the 'most persuasive' case. At the other end we find the academic systems. Capper and Susskind's Latent Damage system exhibits both aspects and would possibly occupy an intermediate position.

However, it seems that there can be no such thing as a purely academic system. Statutory law and precedents could possibly be represented in a computer system by the law-formulations themselves, i.e., as textual documents. However, in all but classical document-retrieval systems we insist on a formalization of the law and the retrieval of cases by conceptual methods. This process must in some way be prescribed by a human expert, and the retrieval will reflect his expertise. Nevertheless, this kind of system is what is usually meant by an academic system. In this latter sense all systems described in chapter three are academic systems.

4.4.3 System Users.

In section 4.3.2 we emphasized the fact that only experiential systems may be considered practical (at the present state-of-the-art). Also formalizations of statutory law could be made into practical systems as explained in section 3.2.2.2. These would then be examples of what Susskind calls "first generation expert systems in law" ([Susskind89a], p.599).

In order to design second generation systems it is important to consider the different kinds of users of legal computer systems and their requirements with respect to the deep/shallow and experiential/academic features. This topic has been dealt with by Bench-Capon in [Bench89].

He distinguishes between two kinds of adjudicators:

"those whose role is to apply the law as set out in the legislation and the decisions of superior adjudicators, and those superior adjudicators whose decisions become, through the mechanism of precedent, the law to be applied by lower adjudicators." ([Bench89], p. 44)

It is widely accepted by jurists that the large majority of cases are 'easy'. This is true in a formal legal domain and perhaps even more so in quasi-legal domains. These 'easy' cases are precisely the ones decided by the 'lower adjudicators' from the above quotation. Such users could be supported by experiential systems and also by academic systems.

However, 'superior adjudicators' need different kinds of systems. Obviously they must be advised about the law itself, so the systems must be academic or have an academic component. They must decide 'hard' cases and their systems therefore also need deep components in order to overcome problems of open texture.

A lawyer advising a client would first of all need the same knowledge as an adjudicator, including a deep component for 'hard' cases. But he would also have need of a shallow experiential system, or perhaps one system combining both academic and experiential approaches. The academic component would supply him with relevant precedents and arguments. The (shallow) experiential component could give practical advice on court procedure, details about judges etc. The use of statistical data and probabilistic methods would then enable him to give his client an estimate of his chances of winning in court. In order to deal with 'hard' cases the system would also need a deep component.

An experiential system may give a single, definite answer, or perhaps several answers graded according to their probability or certainty-factors. An academic system could also be built to supply a single answer in an 'easy' case. As we have seen above for 'hard' cases, there are many aspects of legal reasoning that an academic decision-making system cannot support or carry out at present. Such a system should therefore not come to any conclusions, but present its user with all relevant data, legal background, precedents and argumentation. In other words, such a system should be an *advisory system*, supporting the user in his decision-making activity.

All the previously mentioned statutory and case-law systems are decision-making systems, except HYPO, CABARET and GREBE which are advisory systems carrying out the above mentioned functions.

4.4.4   Difficult Issues.

We shall give some further examples to illustrate the problems that legal systems have difficulties dealing with. The first example is yet another illustration of the problems that facts-driven systems encounter. The second one will show that there are problems related to legal reasoning that no present day system could cope with.

In any legal situation it is of major importance not only to determine the facts of the case but also to focus on the important features. Let us consider two cases taken from Meldman's area.

Case 1: Meldman's system knows that a "Saturday Night Special" is a kind of pistol, but suppose it was a large screw-driver that the defendant was holding in his hand. Could the system know that a screw-driver sometimes also can be a weapon? The answer to this question is yes, if the system has a sufficiently large knowledge-base (kind-hierarchy). Even then, what does 'sufficiently large' mean?

Case 2: Assume that the defendant held a Teddy-Bear in his hand. This in itself seems entirely innocent and certainly not leading up to neither battery or assault. But what if the defendant was standing up and wildly swinging the teddy-bear over his head? A human lawyer would presumably extract the important feature of this situation, which is that the wild swinging - even of a teddy-bear - may cause apprehension.

In section 3.4.1.2 we described Meldman's system and explained how it could establish *intent* from the information that Aaron Aardvark kicked Zachary Zetz *purposely*. But that was precisely because the connection between purpose and intent is a central feature of assault and battery knowledge, and therefore made part of the system. Meldman's system would not be able to deduce intent or apprehension from the wild swinging of the teddy-bear if this specific connection had not been made explicit. This does not seem feasible, for a system-builder would have to anticipate all kinds of facts and *relations* between facts just in case they were needed.

Even if we assume an enormously large knowledge-base there is a certain problem no system can cope with: We could never guarantee that yet another fact, so far absent and irrelevant to all previous cases may not take an all-important significance in the case at hand.

Consider the following example: Clerks adjudicating cases on the heating addition (described in section 1.6.1 and mentioned above) have decided three imaginary cases as follows:

1:    Facts: House is old.   Decision: House is hard to heat.
2:    Facts: House is draughty.   Decision: House is hard to heat.
3:    Facts: House has no loft-insulation.   Decision: House is not hard to heat.

The last decision may at first sight look surprising, but consider the adjudicating clerk's reasoning: "Having no loft-insulation is no excuse, as one may get it for free from the city-council".

Suppose now a new case comes up. A man applies for a heating addition for his fishing hut, on the grounds that it is old and draughty, as indeed it may be. According to cases 1 and 2 the decision should obviously be 'hard to heat'. However, the (imaginary) Social Security and Health Department (SSHD) has an enterprising lawyer, who wants to argue against such a decision.

The lawyer from SSHD might argue that the owner uses the fishing hut only over the weekend and is therefore not entitled to a heating addition. The applicant's lawyer points out, quite correctly, that the law only speaks about the house being hard to heat, not about extent of use as living quarters. Then the SSHD lawyer brings out the decision from case 3. He says that this decision shows that if the resident has no excuse, he gets no heating addition. The applicant's permanent home is nice and warm and he is not forced to go fishing on cold days.

A computer system could never anticipate such line of reasoning. - but then - the case is obviously 'hard'. It is interesting though, that no computer system would notice that. In Meldman's system all cases are 'easy', so obviously a system of his type implemented in this area of law would not discover that the case is hard.

Even Gardner's type of system, while trying to distinguish 'hard' cases, could not catch this one. Only the first two rules would be brought to bear and they have the same conclusion. The system would therefore judge the case 'easy', the house is hard to heat and the applicant is entitled to a heating addition.

In a HYPO-like system there is really no distinction between 'easy' and 'hard' cases. The system would retrieve the first two cases and leave it at that. It is not easy to see what the dimensions would be in this area of law judging just from the few examples we have given (invented), but 'lacking loft insulation' could be one of them. Even if that is so, the third case would not be retrieved.

However, let us assume a decision by the court in favour of the SSDH. Presumably it would then be possible to add a dimension 'having no excuse' to a HYPO-like system.

A GREBE-like system would behave like Gardner's system and HYPO.

We have already argued that the distinction between 'easy' and 'hard' cases is not always of importance. What this example shows is that *all systems* would indicate a definite decision in this case, while the human lawyer actually succeeded in turning the case into one where opposite decisions at least ought to be considered.

There is yet another feature of legal reasoning which we want to illustrate. It shows a further complication and limitation of a legal computer system. Let us first assume that the SSHD adjudicating clerk decided to give a heating addition to the fishing-enthusiast, stating that 'no excuse' is relevant only for loft-insulation.

Next, suppose the following case comes up. The Duke of Marlborough (reputedly one of England's richest men) applies for a heating addition for his residence, Blenheim Palace, on the grounds that it is old and draughty (it is indeed). Again, according to cases 1 and 2 the decision should obviously be 'hard to heat'. The SSHD lawyer argues that the Duke of Marlborough is rich and therefore not entitled to a heating addition. The Duke's lawyer points out that the law only speaks about the house being hard to heat, not about the wealth of the resident.

The SSHD lawyer cannot use the 'no excuse' argument because of the fishing-hut case. He simply states that it is a generally accepted *principle* that rich people are not entitled to social benefits. This may of course be compared to an example often brought by Dworkin (see, e.g., [Dworkin86], p.15-20): The case of Riggs v. Palmer. In this case a heir who murdered his grandfather so that he would inherit under the latter's will was held not entitled to the inheritance, because the court, on the grounds of a general *principle*, found an exception to the apparently applicable rule of inheritance.

This example differs from the previous one. In the fishing-hut case the lawyer's argument depended on an original interpretation of a previous ratio. As we said, no computer system could be expected to anticipate such an approach. In the second case the lawyer appeals, not to a law-statement, but to a principle. It is perhaps not difficult to see how such principles could be incorporated as 'rules' in a rule-based system. However, as Dworkin points out, the principles are *not* rules and should *not* be used in the same manner, so the implementation is not so easy after all. Furthermore, one cannot determine which principles should be incorporated in a computer system and when they should be applied. When describing the Meta system in chapter six we shall return to this issue.

We have here seen two examples that present case-law systems cannot cope with. But neither could we guarantee that a lawyer or judge would have come up with the new argument invented by the lawyer from SSHD, so we can hardly blame a computerized system for not being more sophisticated.

4.4.5   Analogy.

We have mentioned several methods of legal reasoning in this chapter that present-day computer-systems cannot carry out or support. One of the main reasons is that the systems do not support analogous reasoning in the sense usually understood in AI. For a general survey of such methods see, e.g., [Hall89]. Only Meldman's system includes this feature and in a very elementary form.

We discussed, for example, the common legal approach of using a previous case to convince the judge that a certain legal rule was true and ought to be applied in the case at hand. The reason that this rule should be applied is of course that the two cases are analogous in some sense. As we pointed out, they may not have a single common fact, so the Meldman-type of analogy does not work. It seems to be a very difficult problem to build a computer system to determine this type of analogy.

We also gave another example where neither the facts nor the rulings of the old case and the case at hand were related, but a lawyer would bring the old case in order to show that a similar process of reasoning should be applied in the new case. In other words, the facts-situations are not analogous, the rulings are not related but the thought-processes can nevertheless be understood as analogous by a human being. This kind of analogy seems even further away from a computer implementation.

One approach to analogy (as used, e.g., by Meldman) performs a match between features, i.e. basic facts of two cases. The better the match of features the more analogous the two cases are concluded to be. Our two examples above show that such an approach does not go very far. It seems that if humans recognize two cases as analogous despite a dissimilarity of the facts-situations, then there must be some deeper structure of the cases that make them analogous (see [Winston82]).

A paper by Kedar-Cabelli ([Kedar84]) discusses what this deeper structure can be and how a computer system could possibly recognize it. This paper is actually a research proposal, within the framework of TAXMAN II project, and some of the problems raised in the paper are from the area of law. One problem is related to the example by Hart quoted in section 1.6.1. The question is how to recognize that a bicycle is a vehicle for the purpose of the rule forbidding to take a vehicle into a park. A second example problem is related to the Macomber case discussed in section 3.5.1.3. The problem is to recognize the analogy between the Macomber case and the hypothetical unrealized appreciation case, which was one of Justice Pitney's main arguments for not taxing Mrs. Macomber.

According to Kedar-Cabelli the feature to focus on is reasoning from the *purpose* of the law. In the case of a bicycle it would be considered analogous to a car, not because they are both made of metal or both imported from Japan, but because they would both trample over the lawns, pollute the air and destroy the natural habitat of the park. In the second example the Macomber case and the hypothetical case are similar because there are no changes in the rights of the stockholders. However, as Kedar-Cabelli acknowledges, this similarity is not sufficient. It does not explain why 'no change in rights' is a relevant aspect for the purpose of taxability. This example is therefore more difficult than the first one.

The approach that Kedar-Cabelli proposed to implement is to use the purpose of the analogy and a so called domain-theory (a set of rules expressing necessary common-sense knowledge). Given a new case, e.g. about a bicycle, the system should be able to use the purpose of the vehicle-rule and the domain-knowledge to retrieve a case about a car. The conclusion of the system could then be that as the car is a vehicle for the purpose of the particular law so is a bicycle. However, as Kedar-Cabelli acknowledges, it is far from easy to determine what is the purpose of any law or regulation.

Kedar-Cabelli is one of the coauthors of the paper [Mitchell86] which is one of the basic articles on what is called Explanation Based Generalization (EBG). The ideas from her research proposal are here shown as implemented, but *not* in the legal domain. While EBG has been an extremely active area of research in recent years no published results relate to the domain of law. [Ellman89] is a survey of EBG which includes a section on "justified analogy".

A survey of AI research on analogical reasoning and its possible application in the legal domain is found in [Ashley85]. He also describes a hypothetical computer system, its aims and its functions using analogy. Some of the features that do not relate to analogy have been implemented by Ashley himself in HYPO, while other aspects of HYPO are related to a special kind of analogy (see [Ashley90], p.211-215). A recent work on law and analogy is [Bellairs89] which proposes a theory of analogical reasoning related to the conceptual context of the domain. Bellairs has developed a computer system, BRAMBLE, which applies analogical reasoning using contextual relevance in the legal area of corporate acquisitions.

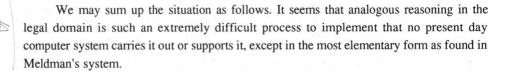

We may sum up the situation as follows. It seems that analogous reasoning in the legal domain is such an extremely difficult process to implement that no present day computer system carries it out or supports it, except in the most elementary form as found in Meldman's system.

4.5 Conclusion.

In this part of the book we have described previous work that relate to legal systems. We have discussed the problems involved and the attempted solutions. However, something fundamental is missing in all existing systems, as their constructors freely acknowledge. The problem of representing the human activity of *actual reasoning* with cases seems to be genuinely difficult. This difficulty is not connected with the problems of how to represent the various kinds of knowledge or what conceptual model to choose and at what level. There is a certain process by which judges decide cases - and by which lawyers reason with cases. A large body of jurisprudence deals with this process. Yet, it seems to be extremely hard to represent and simulate this process within a computer.

We have discussed the problem of retrieving cases. While some methods and principles are obvious, we have pointed out some instances where a human expert would know what precedent to retrieve while the present systems cannot. As for using the retrieved cases for reasoning and supporting the human user the situation is not different. Some features of the process have been implemented but many approaches in legal reasoning have not. As for setting forward a principle (in Dworkin's sense) instead of using a precedent rule - this kind of legal reasoning seems even more complicated than reasoning with previous cases and decisions.

We have already mentioned that other approaches, as yet untried, may be called for. The obvious method which so far is almost unused is analogy. Only Meldman's system uses analogy in a somewhat primitive manner. Analogy obviously has a central place in legal reasoning, but it appears to be extremely difficult to implement this kind of reasoning in a computer system.

There is another problem that we have not considered until now: What kind of user-interface should a legal computer system have. None of the previous systems have developed special interfaces. As we explained in chapter three Meldman's system was planned to execute under the OWL system which was to have a natural language interface, but was completed before this interface was ready. The BNA system has a somewhat user-friendly interface as it uses the query-the-user facility of APES.

It does not seem practical to develop a natural language interface for general use. It may perhaps be feasible for some specific areas. On the other hand, lawyers should not be bothered to learn special interface languages. In our design considerations in the next two chapters we shall take this problem into account.

We have seen the severe problems associated with the facts-driven approach. One of our systems, Meta, actually uses this approach in situations which we believe are justified. However, we shall also propose a different approach in the next part of the book. We shall present the system **JURIX**, which, like HYPO, is an advisory system and does not necessarily distinguish between 'easy' and 'hard' cases. It does not solve the major problems of legal reasoning we have just pointed out, but can be considered as an attempt to give a *practical* method for *advising* lawyers involved in the process of legal reasoning. For **JURIX**-like systems could be built and actually applied in several areas of law without any special difficulties.

PART THREE

The JURIX and Meta Systems:
Conceptual and Implementational Aspects

5

Rule-Guided Analysis

He argued high, he argued low
He also argued round about him.
(W.S. Gilbert, Sir Macklin)

5.1 Introduction.

In the previous chapters we have seen some of the problems that arise when one attempts to build an advisory system for case law. There is the problem of knowledge-representation of common-sense knowledge, cases and decisions. There is the central problem of how to deal with open texture, and - intrinsically connected to that - how to reason with cases. There is the almost untouched problem of dealing with analogous reasoning in law. Finally, we have discussed the jurisprudential concepts of 'easy' and 'hard' cases, we have seen to which extent they are of importance and how previous workers in the field have dealt with them.

We have also discussed various designs for case-law advisory systems and have by now an idea of what we are aiming at. Our first object will be to consider the knowledge sources for our future system, next we shall deal with an appropriate knowledge representation, and finally we shall consider how to utilize the knowledge.

5.2 Knowledge Sources for JURIX.

The obvious sources for our system are of course the case-reports and case-law statements in the particular area of law we shall choose for our work. However, this material has to be organized in some manner.

It does not seem practical to base our system directly on the hundreds, perhaps thousands of case-reports in the chosen area of law. These cases deal with practically all aspects of human activity. In the area of nuisance we have already given examples relating to noise from musical instruments, motors etc. Other activities relate to damages from overflowing water, from pieces of building materials falling off a house etc. One must therefore first look for some way to organize and classify this vast amount of material.

For guidance we may look to the comprehensive treatises written by legal experts. These text-books describe the various elements apparently necessary and sufficient for liability in the particular area of law, possible defences etc.

Some of these text-books are used not only for teaching purposes, but attain a very high degree of authority among legal practitioners. In the area of Torts the book by Prosser ([Prosser41]) is an American authority, while the treatise by Salmond [Salmond87] is a widely accepted authority in England. The latter book has been through nineteen editions, and is cited in hundred of cases in England and the Commonwealth, by both counsel and judges. The original author (Salmond) deceased many years ago and has been followed by four generations of successors. Nevertheless, as a matter of convenience, we shall refer both to the author and to the book itself as Salmond.

While carrying out the research for this book we used the edition: [Salmond81]. A newer edition: [Salmond87] has been published. In the area of nuisance it appears that there are differences between the editions at only a few places. We shall proceed to use [Salmond81], but utilize the appearance of a newer edition to draw some important conclusions later.

Salmond begins his discussion of nuisance by giving a general explanation of this area of law. He explains that liability springs from a condition on the defendant's land and that protection is accorded to the plaintiff's enjoyment of his land. In order to justify such a statement he quotes a judicial definition which has often been cited with approval:

"Private nuisances, at least in the vast majority of cases, are interferences for a substantial length of time by owners or occupiers of property with the use or enjoyment of the neighbouring property." (Cunard v. Antifyre [1933] 1 K.B. 551, 556-557).

The general discussion of nuisance indicates that there are certain major aspects that must be present together in order to create an actionable situation. Salmond proceeds and considers each of these major aspects by itself.

One such major issue is: who can sue in nuisance. In the following we shall for convenience rephrase this as: who is a *competent plaintiff*. Salmond considers this question in detail, as may be seen from the following representative excerpt:

"It follows from what has been said above that the plaintiff must be able to show that he is entitled to the right to enjoyment of land which nuisance protects. That right normally vests in the person in possession of the land injuriously affected.(77) So a weekly tenant (78) or a tenant at will (79) may maintain an action for nuisance, though the duration of the tenancy may be relevant to the question whether and on what terms an injunction should be granted. Conversely, a revisioner has no cause of action unless he can prove a permanent injury to his proprietary right.(80)...." ([Salmond81], p.55).

We notice that each general statement is referenced by at least one specific case (here indicated by reference-numbers) whose ruling supports the general statement. For example, the assertion that a tenant at will is a competent plaintiff refers to the case Burgess v. Woodstock [1955] 4 DLR 615. In this case-report one finds the following statement:

"Since a weekly tenant may maintain an action for nuisance I see no reason why a tenant at will may not also do so." (McLennon J., Burgess v. Woodstock [1955] 4 DLR 615).

We shall give another example of such a major aspect of nuisance cases. According to Salmond there are six categories of *defences*. He discusses each of these categories by itself, again giving general statements supported by references to precedents. One of these categories he calls *reasonable use of property*. As we have already considered examples relating to features of this defence we shall examine what Salmond has to say about it in more detail.

With respect to this issue there are some appreciable differences between [Salmond81] and [Salmond87].

[Salmond81] distinguishes two parts of this defence:

(a) The state of affairs must be, in all circumstances, common and ordinary; and

(b) (i)Where the state of affairs is an activity, that activity must be reasonably undertaken;

(ii)Where the state of affairs is a condition on the land, the failure to prevent the condition's causing harm must be reasonable. ([Salmond81], p.66).

Salmond now considers each of these two parts. We shall quote an excerpt of his discussion of the second part:

"If the defendant has adopted the usual and expected means of proceeding, that will usually be reasonable.(96) An activity may be reasonable if undertaken at a certain time but unreasonable if undertaken at another time.(97)....." ([Salmond81], p.69).

Each reference here points both to cases where the activity was considered reasonable and to cases where the activity was considered unreasonable. However, as Salmond points out:

"If the defendant has acted maliciously, then his act is *ipso facto* unreasonable. This is made clear by *Christie v. Davey* (1) in which the defendant was held liable because his "musical" activities were undertaken maliciously, whereas the plaintiff (the defendant on the counterclaim) avoided liability because her piano playing was performed at reasonable hours for only a moderate length of time each week." ([Salmond81], p.69).

Salmond now goes on and discusses other situations where an activity would be considered reasonable, as always with an appropriate case-reference for each statement. But he also comes up with a statement like the following (which is not referenced by any case):

"The more skill with which a defendant acts, the more likely it is that the court will find his act reasonable."([Salmond81], p.69).

The statement just quoted differs from the previous ones as it does not state a rule but rather seems to give some general advice. We also notice that it is not referencing a specific case. We shall discuss below what position Salmond's statements may have as a basis for a computer system on nuisance. In particular we shall consider this statement.

In [Salmond87] the aspect of 'ordinary state of affairs' does not appear at all. The defence of 'reasonable use of property' is considered less straightforward. As [Salmond87] says:

"If the defendant has created a nuisance, it is actionable; but the "reasonableness" of his conduct is relevant in determining whether he has in truth created a nuisance." ([Salmond87], p.82).

An investigation why such a change has taken place from one edition to the next is a matter for experts in torts and jurisprudence. From our point of view the emphasis should be on the fact that only few changes have taken place over a period of six years.

To summarize, we observe that Salmond (and similar legal authorities) organizes the material in a way that suggests that his treatise may form the basis for a legal advisory system. He classifies the area of nuisance according to some major concepts and issues (who may sue? what is a defence? etc.). Each of these issues he then classifies into sub-issues (a defence can be: ordinary state of affairs plus reasonable activity etc.) and so on.

Even though the book has been through nineteen editions over the years, the changes reflecting new case-law are apparently slow, and the overall organization seems fairly constant. This is probably one of the main reasons why the treatise has gained such an authority among legal professionals.

We may raise the question to what extent the treatise reflects the law of nuisance and can be used as the basis of an academic computer system in this area. In this connection we shall consider the following opinion given by Professor W.L.Twining and quoted in the preface to [Salmond81]:

"the criteria of relevance of *Salmond on Torts* are very close, but not identical, to the criteria of a rather formalistic appellate court judge dealing with questions of law within that general area" ([Twining74]).

If the criteria of "Salmond on Torts" are close to those of a judge the book may obviously be used as a basis for an advisory system. The fact that the judge would be considered rather formalistic would seem very appropriate for use in a computer system which is formalistic by necessity.

Now Twining's opinion (presumably concerning the *formalistic* approach) can be viewed as a criticism, but one of the authors of the present edition of Salmond (R.F.V. Heuring) regards it as complimentary. As he explains:

" While attention has been paid to the social implications of decisions, there are limits to what can be done within the limits of what is intended to be a readable textbook and not a volume in an encyclopedia of the social sciences." ([Salmond81], Preface).

In other words, the fact that Twining thinks that the book is like a *formalistic* judge, is taken by Heuring to mean that it does not consider social implications of decisions. From our point of view this is actually for the best. No existing case-law system has attempted to deal with historical developments, social or economic implications, but only with a pure analysis component of legal reasoning. Meldman states explicitly that this is his purpose, but the others do it tacitly.

In the conclusion of chapter four we considered the possibility of introducing principles (in Dworkin's sense) into a case-law system. This might be appropriate if we want to use Salmond and yet overcome Twining's criticism. But the problem of building case-law systems is extremely difficult. Previous researchers have only taken a few first steps (as they acknowledge) and there are many challenging problems to attack without this additional complication. We shall therefore proceed on the assumption that the treatise by Salmond may form the basis of a case-law system.

5.3 System Design.

We have observe above that a typical legal authority organizes the previous cases in a particular manner, according to certain concepts and abstract issues. If, e.g., we consider the book by Salmond, we would want to represent the information that Salmond has provided in a form which would allow a user to investigate a given case according to Salmond's characterization of nuisance.

For example the statement that a tenant at will is a competent plaintiff may be represented as a 'rule' of the following form:

competent plaintiff **if** tenant at will

If we want to consider the other example (concerning possible defences) we could get the following set of 'rules':

defendant has defence	**if**	state of affairs is ordinary
	and	activity is reasonably undertaken
activity is reasonably undertaken	**if**	means of proceedings is usual or expected
	and	defendant is not malicious

Not all of Salmond's statements can be translated into 'rules' of this kind. We gave an example in the previous section of the following statement by Salmond:

"The more skill with which a defendant acts, the more likely it is that the court will find his act reasonable."([Salmond81], p.69).

It does not seem possible to turn this statement into a rule. As a matter of fact it seems far more appropriate to use such a statement in an experiential system than in an academic one (which it is our aim to build). Such an experiential system may use the above statement to create a rule stating: "If a lawyer wants to show that his client (the defendant) acted reasonably, he should try to show that the client acted skillfully."

This raises the general question to which extent one should consider Salmond's statements as translatable into 'rules' for an academic system or as statements about what evidence is likely to be successful in court proceedings, i.e. material for an experiential system.

As we have just seen, some of the material in Salmond undoubtly relates to an experiential system. However, most lawyers do *not* consider the authoritative textbooks as sources for such systems. Also Twining's statement in the previous section seems to indicate that Salmond primarily attempts to represent the law, i.e. is suitable as a basis for an academic system.

In the area of Artificial Intelligence the concept of heuristics is very central. We may inquire whether this concept also enters our domain. In an experiential system a rule like: "If the judge is old do not bring your client's children to court" would be considered a heuristic rule. In an academic system the rules we have derived from Salmond (or from similar treatises) could be considered heuristics in the sense that they are *not* the law itself but only an approximation of the law. However, in contradiction to the meaning generally used in AI such heuristics have no probabilistic values associated with them.

On the other hand, these rules may change according to future court-decisions. This also means, that they can never be exhaustive. To see this consider for example the rules for 'competent plaintiff'. Let us assume (for simplicity) that there are only two rules:

competent plaintiff	**if**	owner-occupier
	or	tenant of premises

Let now suppose that in a given case we examine the facts relating to the plaintiff. We may conclude that he is neither an owner-occupier nor a tenant of the premises. Nevertheless, it would be *legally wrong* to conclude that the plaintiff was not competent. For we can never foresee what the judge will decide in the case at hand. There may be some circumstance of the case which makes the judge decide that the plaintiff is after all, say, a tenant. It is also possible that the judge will add another category of competent plaintiffs, i.e. it will be necessary to add another rule to the given two.

Our main point is that despite the fact that such 'rules' are approximate only, they form a convenient basis for supporting our reasoning about case-law. How to go about that we shall see in the following.

If we now proceed to interpret Salmond's book (or rather the nuisance part of it) we eventually arrive at the following scheme of logical rules:

nuisance	**if**	competent plaintiff
	and	defendant has no defence
	and	appropriate length of time
	and	liable defendant
	and	.....
competent plaintiff	**if**	owner-occupier of premises
	or	tenant of premises
	or	.....

. . . .

Each antecedent may itself be defined by rules, thus adding a second level of logical structures. We saw this in the previous section with respect to 'tenant', who could be either 'weekly tenant' or 'tenant at will', and also with respect to 'reasonable activity'. We shall here give yet another example: the concept 'appropriate length of time'. Salmond distinguishes several possibilities for the length of time to be appropriate, according to the various cases where this issue was decided. We can therefore have a rule:

appropriate length of time	**if**	action is continuous
	or	action is repetitive
	or	action is intermittent
	or	...

Next we could set about looking for a rule giving conditions for 'action is continuous', for 'action is repetitive', etc. Now Salmond does not give any further rules relating to 'action is continuous'. The reason for that is probably that there are no cases in the law-reports justifying such a refinement, but there are cases where the judge explicitly mentions the concept of a 'continuous action' (for example Cunard v. Antifyre [1933] 1 K.B. 551).

In other words, when lawyers and judges reason about a nuisance case where the issue of time seems relevant they could argue about the concept 'action is continuous'. It therefore seems that 'action is continuous' is an abstraction at the lowest appropriate level.

If, however, a lawyer (and judge) in a new case should decide to descend to a conceptual level even further down than previously done, the present system of logical rules will not be able to cope with it (as we have already remarked). As this feature is very important we shall give two concrete examples of this.

Let us first assume that in a certain case the plaintiff complains of a noise recurring every five hours. According to the existing rules (and statements in Salmond) the relevant issue is 'action is repetitive'. It is in relation to this issue that the lawyers in the case will build their arguments, supported by whatever previous cases have dealt with this issue. Suppose now that the judge finds for the defendant declaring that if the interval between occurrences is greater than one hour it is no nuisance. It will then be necessary to add a further level and perhaps formulate rules like the following:

| action is repetitive | **if** | interval between occurrences less than one hour |

After such a decision also a text-book like Salmond must be updated and mention this new aspect of 'appropriate time' with a reference to the case.

We shall give another, slightly different example of this. Let us refer back to our example of 'hard to heat' from the previous chapter (see section 4.4.3). The situation described after the three cases would give rise to the following system of rules:

hard to heat	if	house is old
	or	house is draughty
	or	house has no loft-insulation

A person applied for a heating addition for his fishing hut, but the lawyer for the SSHD argued against giving such an addition as the fisherman 'had no excuse'. Assume the adjudicating clerk had accepted the 'no excuse' argument in the fisherman's case and denied the heating addition. The set of logic rules stating the conditions for 'hard to heat' would then have to change accordingly. In this case we would not add a level to our rules, but simply exchange one for another.

The new set of rules would then have the form:

hard to heat	if	house is old
	or	house is draughty
	or	applicant has no excuse

We have already pointed out that the authority that Salmond's book has attained relates to the constancy of the scheme of rules originating from it. The kind of rules derived from Salmond will have the same constancy and we propose to base our system upon these rules.

Let us here point out, that the use of rules derived from authoritative treatises is not original. Other system builders have also used text-book rules. Meldman uses [Prosser41], Gardner uses [Fuller72] and HYPO uses [Gilburne82]. However, our proposal is not just to use rules from a treatise, but to apply these rules according to the *special structure* indicated in such a book.

We propose the following design of what we shall call a *concept-driven* system. Using Salmond (or a similar treatise in the appropriate area of law) we formulate a set of logical rules. As we have seen, such rules do not operate with the basic facts of a case (as in a facts-driven system) but use abstractions, general concepts that an authority like Salmond has used to organize the case-law in the particular area.

Obviously these concepts are related to the dimensions of HYPO. From the published documentation about HYPO it seems that a HYPO-like system in the area of nuisance would have some dimensions coinciding with concepts from Salmond, while other dimensions could be composed of several basic concepts from Salmond. But in contradiction to HYPO the kind of system we propose should not begin by collecting basic facts and then compute which dimensions were relevant. We suggest to work straight with the abstractions and let the human user of the system decide whether they are relevant according to the facts of the case (which of course are known to him).

There is a certain danger of over-trivialization of a concept-driven system. One could argue that there is only one relevant abstract concept to consider, i.e. 'nuisance' itself. Thus one could conceivably construct a computer system which began (and ended) by querying the user: "Is it nuisance? Please answer yes or no". Such a trivial system would of course have no practical use.

By choosing Salmond's scheme we have overcome that problem. Salmond relates the top-level concept of nuisance to other concepts (competent plaintiff, no defence etc.). Each of these concept is in its turn decomposed into other abstract concepts. This decomposition stops when a level is reached where the concepts are the ones judges and lawyers actually reason with. While a lawyer may argue in court that a certain activity was continuous he would never walk into the court-room and just state that the activity was a nuisance and then sit down.

We now raise another question related to the structure of the levels of concepts and their associated rules. Would it be possible to find such a refinement of the rules that it would almost never be necessary to change them according to new decisions? Using concepts defined in section 4.3.2 we may relate this to the depth of complexity of the model on which the system is based. The question is whether it is possible to define a sufficiently deep conceptual model which can be used to formulate abstractions with long-range applicability, perhaps in terms of Hohfeldian concepts. This would be in accordance with McCarty's opinion that a deep conceptual model is needed for further development of systems for legal reasoning.

5.4 Rule-Based Execution.

The question is now how to use the derived set of rules. This set of rules may formally be considered as a logic program. If, for example, the facts of a case are given, one could execute this program in Prolog and arrive at an answer: nuisance - or not nuisance. It would make no difference if the necessary data were input initially to the system or elicited from the user by a query-the-user facility (as we pointed out in chapter four).

The data for the program would *not* be the basic facts of the case at hand, e.g. the age of the plaintiff, the fact that he lives at a certain address etc. The basic data would be the *concepts* that appear in the rules at any level: 'competent plaintiff' or 'plaintiff is owner-occupier' etc.

Let us assume that the system uses the query-the-user facility of the APES development system (see [Sergot83], [Hammond83]). The user would be queried: Is the plaintiff owner-occupier? If he answered *no*, the system would ask whether the plaintiff was a weekly tenant, a tenant at will etc. If he answered *yes*, the system would proceed and ask whether the time was appropriate etc.

We have seen a similar kind of system already twice: The BNA system and Meldman's system. As we already explained in the previous cases there are three ways of looking at such a system. (1) The formulation of the rules we use ignore the open texture. (2) The rules express the open texture but the yes/no answers ignore it. (3) The system is appropriate only for 'easy' cases, where the answers indeed are yes/no.

This, however, is not the kind of system we are aiming at. We are interested in a computer system which will give advice to the human user and support him in his reasoning with case-law. We are not interested in a system which supplies yes/no answers. It is interesting, though, to see that using the concept-driven approach, a system may be constructed for case-law which is quite similar to one for statutory-law (BNA).

At this point we must remind ourselves that the rules we apply are derived from an 'authoritative treatise'. Such treatises are undoubtly of central importance in all kinds of legal activities. However, legal experts agree that so-called 'authoritative treatises' actually are not always authoritative in the following sense: (1) Experts may disagree about the extent to which such treatises represent law-statements. (2) A treatise or textbook may have persuasive influence if quoted in court but its holdings are never binding. This means that rules derived from such a 'secondary' source actually may be of dubious validity. This raises a serious question about the applicability of a deductive system based on such rules.

We shall now consider another approach to using the derived rules which overcomes some of the problems raised above.

5.5 Rule-Guided Analysis.

5.5.1 Overview of Method.

In the previous section we saw a use of the 'rules' which was not compatible with our aim of supporting a human user in his reasoning with case-law. We therefore propose to use the general rules derived in section 5.3 in a different manner.

Let us restate the set of logic rules (logic program) and make the basic assumption that they express the open texture of the law. This was one of three possibilities mentioned above.

nuisance	**if**	competent plaintiff
	and	defendant has no defence
	and	appropriate length of time
	and	.....
competent plaintiff	**if**	owner-occupier of premises
	or	licensee of premises
	or	....
defendant has no defence	**if**	....
appropriate length of time	**if**	action is continuous
	or	action is repetitive
	or	action is intermittent
	or	.....

.....

We emphasize that each rule is supposed to express the open texture of the law. It will therefore not always be possible to answer Yes or No when queried, for example, whether the plaintiff is 'competent'. For a given case there may be reasons to conclude that the plaintiff is 'competent', but also reasons to conclude that he is not. Let us now assume that a computer system *indexes* a knowledge-base according to the antecedents (the 'concepts') of the program. This means that for each concept it is possible to retrieve legal information related to this concept, i.e. authoritative quotations, relevant precedents, argumentation etc.

We shall now illustrate the use of the logic program based on the above set of rules. Our aim is to go through what we shall call the *primary issues*, i.e. the concepts appearing as conjunctive antecedents of nuisance itself, i.e. 'competent plaintiff', 'defendant has no defence' etc. For each of them we shall attempt to establish the legal situation of the case at hand, either through a priori, personal knowledge or through legal information supplied by the system. This may sometimes mean that we can give a definite answer, like: "Yes, the plaintiff is competent" or "No, the defendant has no defence". However, there may also be occasions when no such definite answer can be given. In any event, we shall enable the system to retrieve and store all legal material relevant to the issue for later evaluation by the user.

After having considered the legal situation of all primary issues on the advice of the system, the user can then make an overall estimate of his case. He may conclude that it is 'easy' or 'hard' or he may not care to operate with these concepts at all.

Assume the system queries the user about a primary issue, say: Is it true that 'competent plaintiff'? (The complete set of rules for nuisance, based on [Salmond81] may be found in Appendix I). As we have just explained, we can use the concept itself, i.e. 'competent plaintiff', to retrieve decisions from previous cases and learned opinions about this concept. After seeing this information - or part of it - the user may then choose to answer the question, saying Yes or No. (Section 6.6 contains a worked through example of a session with **JURIX**).

An answer of Yes or No means that the issue 'competent plaintiff' was 'easy' in the given case and one should proceed to examine another primary issue. According to the above set of rules this would be: 'defendant has no defence'.

However, suppose the user, after considering the legal information retrieved cannot decide whether the plaintiff is competent, i.e. there may be arguments both for and against such a conclusion, or he simply does not know enough about this concept in relation to the facts of the case at hand. Then the next level of rules could be activated. The system would query the user: [is plaintiff] owner-occupier? Again, the system should enable him to retrieve all relevant legal information about this concept. If he answered Yes, it would mean that the primary issue of 'competent plaintiff' was settled and it would be possible to proceed with the next upper level concept.

If the user answered No (to the question whether the plaintiff was owner-occupier), the system should query him whether [the plaintiff is a] tenant of premises, which would also imply that the plaintiff was competent. If the answer was No also to this question there may be other possibilities (indicated by .... in the above logic program) for a competent plaintiff.

Now suppose the user decides that there are indications that 'plaintiff is competent'. He might possibly be considered a 'tenant', but the user is not quite sure. The system could then descend to a lower level and supply information about weekly tenants, tenants at will etc.

It may also happen that the system while pursuing a certain primary issue has reached the bottom level and the user has not reached a definite Yes or No answer. This means that the particular issue is 'hard'. The system should do nothing else but supply background material for reasoning about the issue.

To summarize: The aim is to use the logic program to go through the primary issues and decide to what extent they have definite answers or not, i.e. whether they are 'easy' or 'hard'. For a given case this may sometimes be possible straight away. If not, it may still be possible by considering low-level rules. Whether a definite answer is possible or not, the system can always supply the user with the appropriate legal material that will enable him to evaluate a particular issue, both at the primary level and at lower levels.

After having processed all primary issues the user now has a picture of the given case. He knows which issues are 'easy' (and also why) and which issues are 'hard'. The system will have supplied him with precedents to use in arguing his case and argumentation both for and against a certain decision.

From the point of view of the system there is really no distinction between 'easy' and 'hard' issues (cases). The system has broken the problem up into several components (primary issues). It can supply argumentation for each of them. It is up to the user to draw whatever conclusion he would like from the retrieved material.

In section 1.7 we described the various steps involved in CBR (Case Based Reasoning). **JURIX** may be characterized as a system which retrieves cases from a case-base using indices defined according to the structure of an authoritative textbook. Thus, while **JURIX** does no reasoning itself, it guides the user in his reasoning according to this structure.

5.5.2 The Associated and-or Tree.

We may associate an and-or tree to the logic program from the previous section:

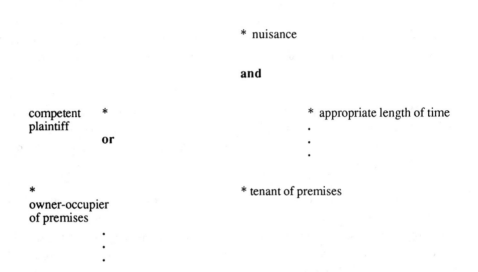

We may explain the execution of the program using this and-or tree. Each node corresponds to a concept in the logic program and each side is labeled **and** or **or** accordingly. The program starts at the root-node (nuisance) and processes the so-called primary-nodes which correspond to the primary issues (competent plaintiff, defendant has no defence, etc.). At each node the user is queried and may answer Yes/No/Maybe.

Consider now nodes (concepts) of the same level connected by the **and** or the **or** operator and forming the antecedent of some higher level node (concept). If the user had answered Yes or No when queried about the higher level node, this particular lower level would not have been reached at all. Suppose therefore that the initial answer for the higher level node was: Maybe. This answer is only temporary and may be changed according to the answers at the lower level which are backed up through the tree. We shall now explain how truth-values are backed up from one level to the next higher one.

Assume first the nodes at the lower level are connected by **and**. If a query related to any of them is answered by No, this will also the backed up value. If all queries are answered by Yes, this will the backed up value. If there is at least one Maybe answer (all other answers being Yes or Maybe) the backed up value is Maybe.

Assume now the nodes are connected by **or**. If any query is answered by Yes, the backed up value is also Yes. If all queries are answered by No, the backed up value is either No or *Maybe*. This may look surprising, but will be explained below. If there is at least one Maybe answer (and all other answers are No or Maybe) the backed up answer is Maybe.

We must explain why the backed up value of all No's yields either No or Maybe. In applied logic we may sometimes make the assumption that anything not known to be true is false. There are many domains where this assumption is acceptable. Were it so in our case, the backed up value after receiving only No answers would also be No. For example, if all the successor-nodes of 'competent plaintiff' (i.e. 'owner-occupier of premises', 'tenant of premises' etc) were false, then we could conclude (using this assumption) that we cannot know whether 'competent plaintiff' was true, and therefore it was false.

However, in law this assumption is not valid. The denial of this assumption is a fundamental characteristic of law closely connected to the open texture of law.

To see that, let us look at the following rule:

appropriate length of time
if	action is continuous
or	action is repetitive
or	action was for short period only
or	action is intermittent
or	action happened on few occasions only
or	action happened on one occasion only

This is the complete rule for the condition: 'appropriate-length-of-time'. Assume now that the user has answered No to all the right-hand side conditions. This still does not mean that the length of time is not appropriate. The interpretation of the rule is only related to categories created by Salmond for previous cases. As we have already pointed out in section 5.3 it does not mean that in a future case these categories are the only relevant ones. In an 'easy' case the backed up answer could be No, if the user was sure about it. If he is not, the backed up value should be Maybe, for we cannot know what decision a judge may reach in a case that has not yet been decided.

The principle we have just applied to or-nodes raises a similar question for and-nodes. Let us reconsider the case of a node whose sons (antecedents) are connected by the **and** operator. Let us assume that the lower level nodes all yield the answer Yes. One may ask why the backed up value of Yes-answers yields Yes (as we stated before) and not Maybe. The reason for this is the *legal* assumption that the given set of relevant and-nodes is *exhaustive*, at least at the level of primary nodes. There is thus no possibility of further antecedents with as yet unknown answers.

However, it is conceivable that the situation could be different at lower levels in our domain (nuisance) or, indeed, at any level in other legal domains. When nodes are connected by the **and** operator the answer to a set of exclusive Yes answers could therefore be either Yes or Maybe.

In the way we have described the program will process all primary concepts, descending into the lower levels of definition only when the user finds it necessary. It will supply legal information whenever requested by the user.

What happens now when the entire set of rules has been processed? The final output should be a summary of the issues found problematic together with the relevant legal information, citing all conflicting and contradictory decisions. If the backed up value to the top rule is Yes or No, the system should point out to the user that the case is 'easy', and it can output the appropriate decision together with all the precedents supporting it.

Let us try to understand what exactly the significance of a Maybe-answer will be. There appear to be three different interpretations:

(1) We do not know what the answer is to the particular question for the given case.
(2) There are reasons to believe that the answer could be *both* yes and no.
(3) We are not sure what can be proven in court with respect to this issue.

The last interpretation is very interesting. It means that our proposed academic system after all has a definite experiential flavour. We have already mentioned the possibility of combining an experiential and an academic system. Perhaps the place to merge academic and experiential knowledge is at each node in the and-or tree. This is the spot where the user asks the system for information, so perhaps he should be supplied with all kinds of knowledge.

We must now deal with the problem of the validity of the rules derived from Salmond. As we pointed out in the previous section the validity of rules derived from secondary sources is dubious, even when such sources usually are considered authoritative.

However, the use of the rules according to our proposal is acceptable. Even if a certain rule is totally wrong in some circumstance it is still of organizational value. It can still be used as a way of *indexing cases*. For obviously a precedent may be very relevant to a given case despite the fact that it is retrieved by a rule which some experts hold to be unacceptable.

This is precisely the point where the case-based paradigm has a clear advantage over the rule-based approach as applied, e.g., in the systems by Meldman and Gardner. For the rationes decidendi used as a source for the rules in those systems are never explicitly stated. The rules will therefore never have the same authority as the cases themselves when retrieved by rule-indices.

Let us note that the system should not stop exploring **or**-nodes in the and-or tree the moment the truth-value Yes is found for any of these nodes. **JURIX** should continue its exploration in such a situation, as indeed any legal system ought to do. Obviously a user is interested in obtaining as many positive approaches and arguments for his side of a given case. These approaches are each characterized by a different or-node with truth-value Yes.

5.6 Evaluation of System.

5.6.1 Comparison with Other Systems.

In the preceding sections we have outlined the structure of a legal computer system based on the knowledge represented in an authoritative treatise and structured accordingly. This system is an advisory system and it confronts the open texture of the law by supplying arguments and precedents both for and against a certain decision.

The system has a certain rigidity: It can approach legal problems *only* according to a Salmond-structure. But legal experts may very well argue that there could be other approaches to a given case. HYPO, for example, operates with dimensions each of which comprises of several 'concepts' from **JURIX**. Sometimes a lawyer would consider such dimensions and not individual concepts like in **JURIX**.

The system may be implemented only in areas where authoritative treatises exist. This is undoubtly the situation in many legal domains. However, sometimes a treatise will lose its authority because of new legislation. Furthermore, in unsettled legal areas, like the one considered by [Mendelson89] (see section 4.3.3) the approach does not work, as treatises are usually written only after some measure of stability has been reached in the case-law relevant to the domain.

The main feature of the system as compared to facts-driven systems is its independence of common-sense knowledge. This arises from the use of concepts to guide the user in his analysis, and leaves him with the interpretation of facts-situations and intentions that other computer systems may not be able to cope with.

We must now make a closer comparison of the proposed system with the existing systems. The way to do that is through a re-consideration of the legal problems we discussed in chapter four.

(1) The Teddy-Bear Case.

A **JURIX**-like system in the area of assault and battery would ask the user about concepts like *intent of defendant* and *apprehension of plaintiff*. Relevant legal material would be retrieved by the system and the user would then have to weigh this material. From the point of view of the system it would make absolutely no difference whether the defendant held a knife, screwdriver or teddy-bear in his hand. The user is the one who will decide what implications it would have if the defendant was swinging the teddy-bear wildly over his head.

The reason why a **JURIX**-like system would cope with this case is of course the total lack of dependence on common-sense knowledge.

(2) The Hard to Heat Cases.

In the previous chapter we pointed out that many legal practitioners would not have come up with the argument supplied by the lawyer from SSDH: The applicant has no excuse. No computer would invent it on its own. However, **JURIX** like HYPO would retrieve all relevant cases and leave it at that. On the face of it most human users would consider those cases and come to the conclusion that the case is 'easy' and that the applicant is entitled to the heating addition.

(3) Analogy Cases.

We discussed previously the use of an apparently unrelated case to argue that a certain rule exists and should be applied to the case at hand. If this case is referenced by Salmond,

JURIX would retrieve it. It does not create analogies by itself.

We also discussed the use of a totally unrelated case to argue that a certain reasoning process should be applied to the case at hand. Again, such a case could be retrieved only if Salmond has used it.

5.6.2 Gardner's Objections.

As we are using the query-the-user approach we must discuss some objections to this approach given by Gardner in her book.

Gardner observes (see [Gardner87], p.60) that asking the user is not suitable for a system which is primarily developed for tutoring students. These are supposed to spot the issues from the facts alone without any help from the system. As she remarks, this approach is equivalent to asking the teacher for help with the test.

With respect to **JURIX** she is quite right in this observation. If the purpose of tutoring is to make the students remember which concepts are involved in a particular area of law, then our proposed system cannot be used. Its aim is precisely to guide the user through these concepts in a structured manner. If, however, the user does not have to prove himself in a formal test, he may use the system to complete his partial knowledge.

However, Gardner has a serious objection to asking the user also in other legal situations:

"A judge does not ask the parties to supply more facts; he decides the case on the evidence given. For someone studying a case already decided, the only available facts are those presented in the opinion. The questions the program might ask, then, do not involve simple facts that the user can readily supply. To decide whether a particular predicate is satisfied is to draw a legal conclusion calling for informed judgment. It might be just this judgment that the user of a consultation system lacks." ([Gardner87], p.60).

Gardner says two things here:

(1) The query-the-user approach does not correspond to a real life situation.

(2) The user should not be forced to draw a legal conclusion calling for informed judgment.

Concerning observation (1):

We must relate Gardner's objection to the kind of user the system is intended for. If he is a lawyer, he will ask his client for more facts all the time. So why should the system not ask him? If the user is an adjudicating clerk dealing with 'hard to heat' cases there is no reason why he should not ask for more facts from the applicant, and similarly the system might ask him. So an advisory system for DHSS could definitely use the query-the-user approach.

Finally consider a system intended for a judge. Let us make the (dubious) assumption that a judge does not ask for more facts. But the lawyers appearing in his court do not restrict themselves to relevant facts only. They supply a lot of background, even some intentionally misleading facts. So a judge needs to select the relevant parts from all this. It is therefore difficult to understand Gardner's objection to supplying more facts, also in this case.

In any case, the system we have proposed does not ask the user for *more* facts. It does not ask the user for facts at all. It asks him about legal concepts. Here Gardner's second observation could be relevant.

The title of Gardner's book: An AI Approach to Legal Reasoning" suggests that her aim is to build a system which mimics the way humans reason about legal problems. It is therefore natural that she does not choose to rely on features that a human legal reasoner can do without. However, we are not attempting to imitate human reasoners in **JURIX**, but rather to support him in his reasoning. The objection is therefore not of relevance to a support system.

Concerning observation (2):

The objection would be legitimate were we to use the rule-based execution approach described in section 5.4. But even then, as we have stressed several times, this approach is applicable for 'easy' cases, i.e. cases where we anyway assume that it is permissible to make definite legal conclusions. However, the basic idea of rule-guided analysis is that the user does *not* have to draw a legal conclusion should he not wish to.

It would seem that the same objection could be made against a system using the facts-driven approach. Inputting a fact, say: "X sent a letter" calls for a legal conclusion as well, for "letter" expresses the open texture of the law just like any other concept.

Finally, our proposed system is *intended* to ask the user sophisticated legal questions. The aim of the system is to support the user in answering these questions, should he choose to.

5.7 System Implementation.

5.7.1   General.

In the previous sections of this chapter we saw the design of a concept-driven system based on logic rules derived from an authoritative treatise. Our object is to build a computer program according to that design. In other words, a program which helps the user to carry out a legal analysis according to the text-book rules. It should go through these rules, retrieve relevant legal information and summarise the legal situation for the user. In this section we shall describe the actual implementation of such a system, called **JURIX**.

As commonly done with expert-systems the program may be divided into two parts: The Inference Engine and the Knowledge Base. We shall describe the two parts below.

5.7.2 System Overview.

The main object of the program is to advise, support and guide the user through the nodes of the fundamental and-or tree defined in section 5.5.2. As may be remembered, the nodes of this tree correspond to the rules created on the basis of a legal authoritative text like Salmond ([Salmond81]).

At each stage the user is presented with a menu stating the set of and-nodes or set of or-nodes he has to deal with. In both cases the user may choose the order in which he examines the nodes. For and-nodes he must go through all of them, while in the case of or-nodes he can state how many and which he wants to deal with.

The object of the user is to prune this tree and determine a subtree which represents the given legal situation. At each node the user is asked a certain legal question by the system. He has to answer YES/NO/MAYBE. Before committing himself to an answer the user may request to see relevant legal information. An answer of YES/NO means that the user has no doubts about the application of the particular rule represented by the given node. In that case the subtree below the node is pruned.

An answer of MAYBE means that the user is not sure about the application of the rule. In that case the system will descend into the subtree, querying the user at each further step, until an answer of YES/NO is given or until the leaf-nodes are reached. If the answer of MAYBE is supplied for a leaf-node no further descent is possible and the significance for the system is that a 'hard' issue has been located. An appropriate message is then output to the user.

The answer supplied by the user is backed up through the tree until the sons of the root (called primary nodes) are reached. Thus eventually all primary nodes are associated with truth-values: YES/NO/MAYBE.

The relevant legal information, especially for a subtree of a primary node with a MAYBE value comprises the advice the system gives the user concerning the related 'hard' question. The appearance of one or more NO answers at the primary nodes means that the case is 'easy' and that the defendant is not liable for nuisance. If all primary nodes are associated with YES answers, the case is also 'easy' and the defendant is liable in nuisance.

If, however, the truth-values are all YES and at least one MAYBE, the case is 'hard'. As we have explained in previous chapters the distinction between 'easy' and 'hard' cases is not always of importance. **JURIX** supplies the user with the legal information relevant to his case and the user can then decide himself how to interpret it.

The entire execution takes place within a loop, thus enabling the user to make different choices of subtrees. Each choice of a subtree corresponds to a different legal approach to the case at hand, or to a hypothetical but related case. At each stage the system will supply the user with an overview and a summary of the information obtained so far.

Both the structure of the knowledge-base and the Inference Engine are independent of the particular legal area chosen. In other words, our system is actually a **shell**, if not for all legal advisory systems, then at least for all the systems relating to legal areas of similar structure to nuisance.

As a matter of fact this shell may be used not only in legal applications, but in any field which has decision problems calling for human discretion, again assuming that the field can be described by the same kind of basic and-or tree.

5.7.3 The Knowledge Base.

The Knowledge Base contains four kinds of information:

1. Nodes of the basic and-or tree.
2. Information consisting of authoritative quotes.
3. Information consisting of rationes, dicta and arguments.
4. Case reports.

The feature common to all information-files is that they are indexed by legal rules. Consider, for example the rule:

competent plaintiff **if** owner-occupier of premises

When a user considers the applicability of this rule he is able to retrieve the above types of legal information relating to this rule. This retrieval can take place from three files which are all indexed by the concept 'owner-occupier of premises'. One file contains authoritative quotes related to the particular concept (here 'owner-occupier of premises), another file contains rationes, dicta and argumentation related to the concept and the third one contains case-reports relevant to the concept.

The general idea behind the establishment of these three files is as follows. At the lowest level the user may want general information only. This is the kind of statements found in textbooks, and it may often suffice to enable him to answer the given question. At a more advanced level the user can get extracts from the case-reports: rationes, dicta and argumentation. This saves him from having to read the entire report, if he does not find it necessary. If, however, he should wish to consider the quotes in their proper context, the full text of the reports themselves are available at the third level.

As a matter of principle the exact legal contents of these files is not of great importance. Any system-builder implementing a **JURIX**-like system in another legal area can make his own choice. Also the number of levels (three) could possibly be changed for a different application.

It appears that most of the primary concepts are not referenced in Salmond by any specific cases. These nodes are therefore not connected with three knowledge-files, but only with the one file that contains authoritative quotes.

5.7.4 The Inference Engine.

The program is written in Prolog, but could just as well be written in any procedural language. We shall show the basic algorithm of the inference engine in a Pascal/Ada-like formalism that many people are accustomed to.

WHILE user is still interested LOOP

  -- each iteration of this loop corresponds to a new consideration of the case at
  -- hand, i.e. trying out a new approach, concentrating on another issue,
  -- looking at a hypothetical related case, etc.

  WHILE unprocessed primary nodes left LOOP

      choose a primary node pn;
      -- pn is a primary concept (like competent plaintiff, appropriate time)
      retrieve legal background relevant to pn (if user chooses to);
      collect legal information for summary at end of processing;
      ask user for truth-value of pn;
      IF *yes* or *no* THEN update lists of primary nodes according to their
        truth-value;
           GOTO END of LOOP; -- over primary nodes
      END IF;
      IF *maybe* THEN show son-nodes;
           let user choose subset of relevant son-nodes;
           -- not all sons are relevant for given case
           WHILE set of son-nodes not empty LOOP
           choose son-node: sn;
           PROCESS sn and its sons etc. recursively as follows:
           retrieve legal background relevant to sn;
           collect legal information for summary at end;
           ask user about truth-value of sn;
           IF *yes* or *no* THEN back truth-value up to pn; END IF;
           IF *maybe* THEN process son of sn (recursively); END IF;
           IF bottom level THEN back *maybe* up to father; END IF;
           END LOOP;   -- over set of son-nodes
      END IF;

  END LOOP;   -- over primary nodes

  show legal summary, final truth-values of primary nodes etc;
  ask user if he wants to try another approach;

END LOOP;   -- over different approaches

All technical details of the program have here been ignored, but may easily be reconstructed.

The inference engine is in no way dependent on the particular area of law that we have chosen. It only assumes the basic structure of the data described above.

Some of the predicates responsible for the man-machine interface are of course written with the assumption that the advisory system will function in the legal domain. Our system is thus a general **shell** in this domain. The changes necessary to convert the system from the legal domain to any other domain (assuming the same problem-solving approach may indeed be applied) are quite localized.

5.7.5   Summary.

The program is written as a main loop, enabling the user to run through it as many times as he chooses. In each pass he may want to make certain changes in some of his answers, and retrieve additional legal information. This looping can be understood in several ways.

(1) The user may not always be able to focus on the exact activity that gives rise to nuisance.
(2) A human lawyer may try different approaches to the case at hand. When using the system this is also equivalent to going through several iterations of the main loop.
(3) Sometimes features interact (as in HYPO's dimensions). **JURIX** has no such structure and the user must deal with a possible interaction by looping through the system (backtracking) and change his answers.
(4) This may support the human user in trying out various *hypothetical* situations, as is commonly done by lawyers.

At the termination of the looping the summary can help the user in the writing of a lawyer's opinion.

5.8   Conclusion.

We have proposed a case-based system which differs from other case-law systems primarily in its independence from common-sense knowledge. This is achieved by using what Susskind calls a 'top-down' approach (see section 2.2.2) while others use a 'bottom-up' approach.

The system is an advisory system and behaves like HYPO in retrieving cases though it does not weigh them and does not create argumentation. It thus supports the user who makes the decisions himself.

It is not surprising that we have not succeeded in overcoming the many problems raised in chapter four. As we have already said: The domain of legal computer systems for case-law is very difficult. Our system uses a different approach than other systems, but this does not necessarily mean that it can overcome the problems they failed to cope with. One should consider all present systems, including **JURIX**, as first steps only towards real solutions.

6

The Meta System

The Proof of the Pudding is in the Eating.

6.1 Introduction.

In this chapter we shall consider a certain approach to legal reasoning about case-law, which seems to be applicable to certain quasi-legal areas. We shall describe the design and implementation of a computer system, Meta, which is based upon this approach. We shall also attempt to compare the system with the other case-law systems which we have discussed previously.

The particular quasi-legal area which we have used for implementation of the system has been described in section 1.10.1. It relates to the advisory activity during student registration. A student advisor may sometimes decide to permit a student to register for a certain course without having passed the appropriate prerequisite course. His decision is based on similar precedents and the problem we shall consider below is how to simulate his reasoning with such precedents.

This problem may be compared with the 'hard to heat' problem mentioned several times previously. Both problems have a feature which distinguish many quasi-legal domains from actual legal domains: The relatively small amount of common-sense knowledge needed to characterize the quasi-legal area. It is this feature which will enable a computer system to reason *exhaustively* about the previous decisions and suggest their potential application and weight in a new case.

Meta is based on the idea proposed in [Bench88] (see section 3.5.2). The authors of that paper propose a rule-based treatment of open texture that we have adopted and extended. They state that several rules may be derived from a single precedent, but they do not indicate how these rules should be constructed. Neither do they discuss how the rules should be weighed. The central feature of their approach is their observation that conflicting rules could - or actually must- be included in the knowledge-base in order to express the open texture.

In the rule-based paradigm one would actually apply the rules derived from the precedents. However, as already pointed out in the previous chapter on **JURIX**, rules may be used as indices in the case-based paradigm. This is the approach also used in Meta.

6.2 The Meta-Rule Approach.

6.2.1 Introduction.

When a precedent is given it is not always clear precisely how it should be used with respect to a new case. Authorities usually agree that a rule (called the ratio decidendi) may be formulated based on the precedent, but it is not always clear how this rule should be formulated or used. We shall here consider some of those uses which are met with general acceptance. For a discussion of the use of precedents in the legal domain see [Llewellyn60] and [Cross77].

We shall show how legal reasoning may be simulated by using new rules created by certain *meta-rules* applied to the ratio decidendi. We shall develop these meta-rules through illustrative examples taken from our academic application area. The original rule and the created rules will be used as indices to retrieve relevant cases. We shall also show how a weighting scheme is induced in a natural way by applying the meta-rules.

6.2.2 Derivation of Meta-Rules.

Meta-Rules 1-2.

Assume that a student who belongs to a special study scheme (let us call it scheme_1, e.g. an Honours Course) wanted to register for the course: Theory of Algorithms (called algorithms for short) without having passed the prerequisite course: Data Structures (called structures below). Let us further assume that the advisor permitted this. The obvious rule to be extracted from this case is that any student (say S) belonging to scheme_1 would also obtain a similar permission with respect to the same course. Expressed in clause-form this rule becomes:

permit(S, algorithms, structures) **if** belongs(S, scheme_1)   (1)

Assume now that another student were to make the same application to an advisor (possibly the same one) at a later stage. If the student does not belong to scheme_1 the advisor *may* deny him permission citing the above case and arguing that the correct rule to be extracted from it is:

$\neg$ permit(S, algorithms, structures) **if** $\neg$belongs(S,scheme_1)   (2)

We here use general logic notation for clarity: $\neg$ denotes negation and $\wedge$ will denote conjunction.

Thus in a future, similar case *both* of the above rules should be considered by the advisor. This will enable us to capture the essence of the concept of open texture as described in section 1.6.

The rule (2) can be created automatically by a system using (1). In fact, we may generalize such a process in the following way. Assume: 'p **if** q' is a given rule. The system automatically creates another rule using the following meta-rule (using ==> for meta-implication):

'p **if** q' ==>   '$\neg$p **if** $\neg$q'   (3)

A more general form of this meta-rule could be:

$$\text{'p if } q_1 \wedge \ldots \wedge q_i \wedge \ldots \wedge q_n\text{'} \quad ==> \quad \text{'}\neg\text{p if } q_1 \wedge \ldots \wedge \neg q_i \wedge \ldots \wedge q_n\text{'} \tag{4}$$

However, we have to be careful and distinguish between 'positive' conditions in the antecedent that contribute to convince the advisor to grant a permission and 'negative' conditions which contribute to a decision denying a permission. Only 'positive' conditions may be negated as in (4), while 'negative' conditions may not be negated.

To see this, assume that the student that applied for permission to take algorithms belonged to scheme_1 but had actually failed the structures course. If the advisor nevertheless allowed him to take algorithms we would have the following rule:

$$\text{permit(S, algorithms, structures)} \textbf{ if } \text{belongs(S, scheme\_1)} \wedge \text{failed(S, structures)} \tag{5}$$

There are no problems with applying meta-rule (4) with respect to the first , 'positive' antecedent. However, applying the meta-rule with respect to the second, 'negative' antecedent gives:

$$\neg\text{permit(S, algorithms, structures)} \textbf{ if}$$

$$\text{belongs(S, scheme\_1)} \wedge \neg\text{failed(S, structures)} \tag{6}$$

The rule (6) is patently absurd. The reason for this is of course that the advisor permitted the student to take algorithms *because* he belonged to scheme_1 (a 'positive' condition) *despite* the fact that he failed the structures course (a 'negative' condition).

Denoting 'positive' conditions by q and 'negative' conditions by r we thus get the final form of our meta-rule:

$$\text{'p if } q_1 \wedge \ldots \wedge q_i \wedge \ldots \wedge q_n \wedge r_1 \wedge \ldots \wedge r_m\text{'} \quad ==>$$
$$\text{'}\neg\text{p if } q_1 \wedge \ldots \wedge \neg q_i \wedge \ldots \wedge q_n \wedge r_1 \wedge \ldots \wedge r_m\text{'} \tag{M1}$$

where only the q's may be negated.

Consider now a student who belongs to scheme_1 and has not failed structures. This means that he may never have registered for structures or he may have registered but not attempted to take the final examination. If he had actually passed structures, there would of course be no need to apply for a special permission to take algorithms. He can use (5) to argue (strongly) that he should also be permitted to take algorithms. In other words, the correct form of (6) as obtained from (5) should actually be:

permit(S, algorithms, structures) **if**
$$\text{belongs(S, scheme\_1)} \wedge \neg\text{failed(S, structures)} \qquad (7)$$

which gives rise to the following meta-rule:

$$\text{'p \textbf{if} } q_1 \wedge \ldots \wedge q_n \wedge r_1 \wedge \ldots \wedge r_m\text{'} ==>$$
$$\text{'p \textbf{if} } q_1 \wedge \ldots \wedge q_n \wedge r_1 \ldots \wedge \neg r_i \wedge \ldots \wedge r_m\text{'} \qquad (M2)$$

Meta-Rules 3-4.

In order to develop additional meta-rules assume that some student who belongs to scheme_1 wants to take course_1 (different from algorithms) before having passed the prerequisite course_0. He may argue that our first case indicates that this should be permissible, as the rule derived from it should actually be:

permit(S, course_1, course_0) **if** belongs(S, scheme_1) $\qquad (8)$

Many such rules may be derived using particular knowledge about our domain and common-sense knowledge. For example a student belonging to study scheme_2 may argue that the rule should be:

permit(S, algorithms, structures) **if** belongs(S, any_kind_of_special_scheme) $\qquad (9)$

Rules (8), (9) and similar ones may be obtained from the following meta-rule:

$$\text{'p \textbf{if} q' } ==> \text{ 'p \textbf{if} Q'} \qquad (10)$$

here Q is a condition similar to q in some sense, as in the above two examples. This meta-rule is generalized in the following way:

$$\text{'p \textbf{if} } q_1 \wedge \ldots \wedge q_i \wedge \ldots \wedge q_n \wedge r_1 \wedge \ldots \wedge r_m\text{'} ==> \text{ 'p \textbf{if} } q_1 \wedge \ldots \wedge Q \wedge \ldots \wedge q_n \wedge r_1 \wedge \ldots \wedge r_m\text{'} \qquad (M3)$$

and:

$$\text{'p if } q_1 \wedge ... \wedge q_n \wedge r_1 \wedge ... \wedge r_i \wedge ... \wedge r_m' \implies \text{'p if } q_1 \wedge ... \wedge q_n \wedge r_1 \wedge ... \wedge R \wedge ... \wedge r_m' \quad \text{(M4)}$$

where Q is derived from q_i and R is derived from r_i by generalization/analogy as exemplified above in (8) and (9). For the sake of symmetry we have here distinguished between 'positive' and 'negative' conditions, although the meta-rules M3 and M4 can actually be expressed in a unified form.

Meta-Rules 5-6.

In order to derive our next meta-rules consider the following rule which we assume has been obtained from a concrete case:

permit(S, algorithms, structures) **if** pregnant(S)∧children(S,3)∧failed_courses(S,0)   (11)

Another student with three children who has never failed a course but who is *not* pregnant may have a good argument when asking for permission and using (11) to derive the following rule:

permit(S,algorithms, structures) **if** children(S,3)∧ failed_courses(S,0)   (12)

We therefore formulate the following meta-rules:

$$\text{'p if } q_1 \wedge ... \wedge q_{i-1} \wedge q_i \wedge q_{i+1} \wedge .. \wedge q_n \wedge r_1 \wedge ... \wedge r_m' \implies$$
$$\text{'p if } q_1 \wedge ... \wedge q_{i-1} \wedge q_{i+1} \wedge ... \wedge q_n \wedge r_1 \wedge ... \wedge r_m' \quad \text{(M5)}$$

$$\text{'p if } q_1 \wedge ... \wedge q_n \wedge r_1 \wedge ... \wedge r_{i-1} \wedge r_i \wedge r_{i+1} \wedge ... \wedge r_m' \implies$$
$$\text{'p if } q_1 \wedge ... \wedge q_n \wedge r_1 \wedge ... \wedge r_{i-1} \wedge r_{i+1} \wedge ... \wedge r_m' \quad \text{(M6)}$$

i.e. one of the 'positive' or 'negative' conditions of the antecedent may be deleted. We have here distinguished between meta-rules for 'positive' and 'negative' conditions not only for reasons of symmetry but especially because of the different weightings these rules induce (as we shall see in 6.3).

Note that the consequent rules in M1 and M2-M6 may conflict with each other. As we have emphasized previously this is quite acceptable: It catches the adversarial nature of legal reasoning.

Some expert systems in other domains (but not in the legal area) have used methods equivalent to one or more of the meta-rules M2-M6 but using different points of view. The use of the meta-rules M1-M2 is uniquely connected with the legal (and quasi-legal) domain.

6.2.3 Additional Meta-Rules.

It seems natural to inquire if other meta-rules exist. Two such candidates could be:

$$\text{'p if } q_1 \wedge \ldots \wedge q_n \wedge r_1 \wedge \ldots \wedge r_m\text{'} \quad == > \quad \text{'p if } q_1 \wedge \ldots \wedge \neg q_i \wedge \ldots \wedge q_n \wedge r_1 \wedge \ldots \wedge r_m\text{'} \qquad (N1)$$

$$\text{'p if } q_1 \wedge \ldots \wedge q_n \wedge r_1 \wedge \ldots \wedge r_m\text{'} \quad == > \quad \text{'} \neg p \text{ if } q_1 \wedge \ldots \wedge q_n \wedge r_1 \wedge \ldots \wedge r_m\text{'} \qquad (N2)$$

However, there seems to be neither a formal legal nor an intuitive reason for including these meta-rules.

6.3 Weighting of Rules.

As the meta-rules may be applied over and over again it would seem that the amount of created rules (and hence retrieved cases) could become absurdly great. Also, reapplying M5-M6 could lead to an empty antecedent! However, we have yet to specify how to determine the weights of consequents in the meta-rules given the weights of the antecedents.

Our basic approach to weighting is to define several, discrete levels of weights: e.g. strong, intermediate and weak. The weight of a (manually) defined rule based on a concrete precedent will be assumed always to be at the middle level. Let us now see what should happen when we apply meta-rules. An intuitively correct approach is the following: The further away we go from the original rule (the ratio decidendi) by applying meta-rules the less confidence we have in the derived rules. The weight of a consequent in a meta-rule is therefore determined as one level *below* the weight of the corresponding antecedent. However, this cannot be true for meta-rule M2. The consequent should here have a weight one level *above* the weight of the antecedent rule. The reason for this is of course that the negation of a 'negative' condition in the antecedent of a rule makes us more confident of the applicability of the rule.

The general approach of decreasing the weight with each application of a meta-rule will neither be true in all cases where we apply meta-rules M3-M4. To see this consider the following concrete case: A student applied for permission to take algorithms despite the fact that he failed structures. As the reason for his failure he mentioned that his grandfather had passed away a short while before the test. Let us assume that the advisor granted him permission and we thus get the following rule:

permit(S, algorithms, structures) **if** failed(S,structures)∧deceased(grandfather, S)   (13)

Two similar conditions in the antecedent could be: deceased(father, S) and deceased(uncle, S). In each of those cases we could apply M4 to (13). Now, a student whose father had passed away would presumably have a stronger argument than a student whose grandfather had deceased, and the application of M4 should thus *increase* the weight of the consequent of the meta-rule. On the other hand, a student whose uncle had passed away would have a weaker argument than a student whose grandfather had deceased, and the application of M4 should therefore *decrease* the weight of the consequent in this case.

It may happen that the system derives the same (final) rule in different ways and with different weights. This is quite acceptable. It simply means that there may be several arguments for (or against) a certain decision, some weaker and some stronger. An advisor or adjudicating clerk should of course take them all into account.

The finite, possibly small, number of weight-levels determine the number of times the meta-rules may be re-applied. We shall not allow the application of a weight-decreasing meta-rule to a rule which already has minimal weight. Similarly we shall not allow the application of a weight-increasing meta-rule to a rule which already has maximal weight. Finally, we shall disallow a reapplication of meta-rules M5-M6 when an empty antecedent would have been obtained.

The limitations just stated are usually not sufficient to keep the number of retrieved arguments and cases low enough for the user to survey during the advisory session. It appears that a practical implementation of Meta needs an additional tuning which depends on the particular area of implementation. This tuning will determine the number of weight-levels, the number of allowed iterations for each meta-rule etc.

6.4 Evaluation of System.

6.4.1 Comparison with other Systems.

In section 5.6.1 we compared the **JURIX** system with the other existing systems.

We shall now carry out a similar comparison with respect to Meta.

With respect to common-sense knowledge we observe that Meta is a facts-driven system. It therefore has the obvious disadvantages of such systems if implemented in a general area of law. However, as we have already pointed out, it may profitably be used in a quasi-legal area. These areas often need only a limited amount of common-sense knowledge, and a computer system may therefore reason exhaustively based on its built-in common-sense knowledge.

Thus, a Meta system in the area of assault and battery would not know how to deal with the Teddy-Bear case (from section 4.4.4) if the system-builder had not specifically anticipated such a situation. However, in the 'hard-to-heat' area the system could reason about most if not all cases.

Nevertheless, Meta would not have been able to come up with the 'no excuse' argument supplied by the SSDH lawyer in the fishing hut case (section 4.4.4). Assuming a case-base consisting of the three cases from section 4.4.4 the fishing hut case would be considered 'easy', as no conflicting arguments would be produced by the meta-rule M1.

One may characterize Meta as a Meldman-type system with respect to analogy. We have already said that Meldman's approach is too elementary for a proper legal domain. However, in many quasi-legal areas this approach, as exemplified by meta-rules M3 and M4, will suffice.

It is possible to give a quite different interpretation to the use of meta-rules. We recall Layman Allen's example in section 3.2.2.3. A rule: "Books should be returned by the date due" was interpreted in at least seven different ways. The application of meta-rule M1 corresponds to a *structural interpretation* different from the original one

It is said that any lawyer can turn an 'easy' case into a 'hard' one, should he wish to do so. The legal reasoning simulated in Meta may be interpreted as an attempt to do this, principally by applying the meta-rule M1. Such an approach is not always an advantage and it should not be overdone. This means that the meta-rules should not be applied indiscriminately and the tuning of the system should be done carefully with the aim of reducing the number of retrieved precedents to a minimum.

6.4.2 Additional Rules.

An enterprising applicant (or his energetic lawyer, if the case is actually taken to court) may come up with an entirely new aspect, never considered before. He could argue that students with blond hair and blue eyes should be permitted to take algorithms without having passed structures for some reason which he considers extremely pertinent. In other words, he proposes to add a new case and rule. Obviously the system could not cope with that, as the knowledge-base would not know about students having blond hair and blue eyes.

This does not seem a great problem: We have already emphasized that the common-sense knowledge in quasi-legal domains is very small. Thus chances are that if blond hair and blue eyes is indeed relevant to student registration it would have been discovered long ago and therefore already be part of the built-in knowledge-base. This should be seen in contrast to the real legal world where new facts, new aspects and new approaches are continuously being generated. In any case, the final result should simply be to add the new case and decision (should the advisor accept the argument) to the system.

Consider now another argument (by an enterprising applicant) that the basic rule 'p **if** q' should never have been formulated in the first place with respect to a given case, but that it should have been, say 'p **if** s'. This happens in a real legal domain where a judge may accept a reformulation of the original ratio decidendi. A computer system would not be able to foresee such a situation, but again, it usually does not happen in a quasi-legal domain.

As a conclusion we may say that no computer system could possibly exhibit the kind of originality discussed above. But then, neither would most human beings, including lawyers and judges.

6.5 The Meta **Implementation.**

6.5.1 The **Knowledge-Bases.**

The system knowledge base consists of four parts: The domain knowledge-base (DKB), the common-sense knowledge-base (CSKB), the case-base (CB) and the rule-base (RB). The knowledge representation uses Prolog-rules (Horn clauses). It could equally well be represented by a semantic network or by frame structures.

1. The domain knowledge-base (DKB) for the academic advisory problem contains knowledge about courses, prerequisites, corequisites, requirements for graduation etc. This knowledge is expressed as Prolog-rules, almost all of them in the form of facts. For example:

prerequisite([1989, complex-functions, math-minor], [Year, calculus, Level]).

means that a calculus course taken in any year and at any level is a prerequisite for students studying mathematics as a minor and wanting to register in 1989 for a complex-functions course.

2. The common-sense knowledge-base (CSKB) we have created for the system contains knowledge in Prolog-clause form concerning the world of students, courses, professors, etc. It contains information on departmental and general university policy concerning students. For example, students who have high grades should be encouraged. Students who belong to special groups or special study schemes (usually because they are known to be talented or have a professional background) are also encouraged. The department encourages good students to go to graduate school by allowing them to take graduate courses while still studying for their B.Sc. One aspect of such encouragement is by permitting registration to courses before satisfaction of the appropriate prerequisites. On the other hand, students with bad grades are discouraged from taking too heavy a study-load, i.e., the regulations concerning prerequisites are strictly enforced. However, such students can often appeal to special extenuating circumstances (illness, pregnancy, problematic social background etc.) when applying for special consideration during course-registration. CSKB knows about such circumstances.

There is no clear border between knowledge belonging to DKB and knowledge stored in CSKB. Many items could equally well be defined in either of these knowledge bases.

In both knowledge-bases concepts form tree-like structures. This is necessary in order to determine similarity between concepts by generalization/analogy and also to determine whether to increase or decrease the rule-weight when applying meta-rules M4 and M5.

3. The case-base (CB) contains about 50 *representative* case-descriptions. The initial number of cases was much larger. After some practical use it was decided to reduce the number of cases drastically, as the number of retrieved cases was too great and often had no significance. Each description defines the particular problem (prerequisite and wanted course), the student's background, the advisor's decision and the reason for that decision (exceptionally brilliant student, previous bad record etc.).

4. The rule-base (RB) consists of manually extracted rules corresponding to the cases in CB.

6.5.2   Execution.

The system is designed to be used interactively during registration. Facts are introduced from a student data-base and by the advisor himself. The system uses a special rule generator-and-selector which uses the meta-rules (in a backwards manner) to create applicable rules (some of which may be conflicting) and retrieve their corresponding precedents. Finally the system outputs weighted arguments for and against granting a permission.The argument is in the form of an explanation based on the applied meta-rule(s) and specifies the precedent it is originally based on.

After considering all the arguments the advisor makes his decision. He may also decide that the case at hand and his decision relating to it contribute something new and original, and he will then be requested to formulate an appropriate rule to be added to the rule-base.

6.6.   Conclusion.

The basic idea of the system is the use of several, possibly conflicting rules to express the open texture. Apart from the principal rule (the ratio decidendi) which is extracted manually from a given precedent the system uses built-in meta-rules to create additional rules. This procedure simulates the way a human being would reason if making an application and looking for some justification not derivable in a direct manner from a precedent. An applicant would probably only bring arguments in his own favor. However, the system will also create arguments for the opposite decision. A fair judge or adjudicating clerk should indeed consider all such arguments before making his decisions.

Some of our design decisions may possibly be domain dependent and necessitate some changes if the system is to be implemented in another domain (tuning). The central feature, however, of all such systems is their dependence on a common-sense knowledge-base of manageable size, which enables exhaustive reasoning about a given case.

No deductive process is carried out by Meta using the original or created rules. As in the case of **JURIX** the rules are used as indices to the case-base. The additional features here are:
(1) the simulated reasoning with the rules (i.e., with the retrieved cases) and
(2) the corresponding weighting.

7

Conclusions and Future Work

> When all is said and done, there's a
> lot more said than done.

In this book we have discussed some of the problems that relate to the building of legal computer systems for case-law. It appears that the problem of giving practical advice on case-law is very difficult, and other existing systems are a long way from providing a *practical* aid (as their developers admit). We believe that a simple approach is more realistic. Such an approach is exemplified in **JURIX**. Alternatively, we believe that another kind of system for simulating legal reasoning is appropriate in quasi-legal domains, as exemplified in Meta.

While some researchers have also extracted rules, they have used them *deductively*. We do not apply the rules in such a manner but use a fundamentally different approach, based on the CBR paradigm. **JURIX** provides what we have called a *rule-guided analysis* of a given case, and Meta uses meta-rules to create additional and sometimes *conflicting* rules to be used as indices to relevant cases.

We shall here summarize the problems we have encountered, draw our relevant conclusions and also propose some directions for future research. These research suggestions certainly do not cover the entire area of computer systems for case-law. They should be considered as interesting and important issues which came up during our research and which warrant further investigation.

1. Academic v. Experiential Systems.

We have distinguished between two kinds of systems: experiential and academic ones. Most of our discussion has been relevant to academic systems, but many aspects of experiential systems have also been dealt with. Despite the differences between the two kinds of systems (which we have stressed several times) it seems that there nevertheless are some surprising connections between them.

For example an answer of Maybe to the query: Is the activity reasonable? in the **JURIX** system (see section 5.5.2) can be interpreted as belonging in an academic system and signifying that there are reasons for arguing that the activity is reasonable but also reasons for arguing that it is not. The same answer can also be interpreted as having experiential significance, meaning that it may be possible to prove in court that the activity is reasonable.

Research Problem One: We believe that the interrelationship between experiential and academic systems is an important topic for future research. A good point to start such an inquiry could be an attempt to merge an academic system of the **JURIX**-type with an experiential system in the same area of law.

2. What Kind of System to Aim For?

We have excluded any discussion of the role of evidence in a legal computer system, despite the fact that evidence is of central importance in many areas of law. Also rhetoric and methods of argumentation have not been considered sufficiently in the area of law. HYPO generates argumentation and [Marshall89] discusses the applicability of the ideas of Toulmin (see [Toulmin58], [Toulmin72], [Toulmin79]). Other relevant work in jurisprudence is: [Perelman63], [Perelman69], [Perelman82] and in general AI: [Reichman-Adar84], [Birnbaum80], [Birnbaum82], [McGuire81], [Dyer85] and [Flowers82]. It seems that sufficiently many problematic issues must be faced before dealing with such further complications.

Research Problem Two: To apply existing ideas from Philosophy, Jurisprudence and

Artificial Intelligence concerning rhetoric and argumentation to legal computer systems.

We have emphasized the fundamental concept of open texture in law and discussed its central role in determining the form of a case-law system. Our conclusion has been that the kind of system to aim for is not a system giving definite answers, but rather an *advisory system* aiding the user and retrieving legal information to support his legal reasoning.

In order to get an idea what kind of requirements to formulate for a case-law system, a major part of the book has dealt with previous work. We have considered both systems for statutory law (insofar they were relevant to our topic) and for case-law. We have also considered legal information retrieval systems and their relation to our kind of system. Also some proposals of theoretical nature for dealing with open texture have been examined.

Research Problem Three: [Bench88] describes an approach to open texture which we have extended and implemented in Meta. This raises an interesting question: Is it possible to expand the use of meta-rules to legal reasoning in general?

Research Problem Four: McCarty's theory of Prototypes and Deformations has so far only had a partial computer implementation. This theory has a central role in the understanding of certain types of legal reasoning and ought to have a complete implementation.

The conclusion of our examination of previous case-law systems is that this area is extremely difficult. Existing systems (including our own systems) should only be considered initial attempts (as all system-builders acknowledge themselves). It appears that legal reasoning is a human activity of great complexity and depth, which present day computer systems cannot simulate.

One of the reasons that building case-law systems is genuinely hard relates to the concept of analogy. Analogous reasoning appears to be a central part of legal reasoning and analysis. While humans know how to engage in this activity, computers do not. To give a concrete example (from section 4.4.4): A legal expert will often exhibit an example-case in order to convince a judge that a certain rule applied in that case should also be applied in a new case. The two cases may not have a single common *fact*. Nevertheless, the analogy between the cases will often be realized immediately by humans, while we do not know how to make computers discover it.

Research Problem Five: Future research on analogy in legal computer systems will be of the greatest importance for raising the sophistication of such systems above the present, not very advanced level.

Another problem which dominates existing (facts-driven) systems relates to the relatively small amounts of common-sense knowledge such systems include. Owing to this limitation these systems cannot deal with a very extensive set of problems, but only with such new cases that are related to facts recognizable by their knowledge-bases.

However, problems in quasi-legal areas are often characterized by their dependence on a very limited amount of common-sense knowledge, For that reason it seems to be possible to reason *exhaustively* about such problems.

Research Problem Six: How to cope with the large amounts of common-sense knowledge needed in facts-driven legal systems.

3. Our Design.

In order to evade problems related to common-sense knowledge we have suggested an approach which differs from the previous, facts-driven approach. Our system, **JURIX**, uses a concept-driven approach and needs no common-sense knowledge. These two approaches correspond to what Susskind has called 'bottom-up' and 'top-down' approaches.

While other system-builders have extracted rules from authoritative treatises we have used not only such rules, but also the special structure and organization of the rules found in a text-book. According to the general concepts used in a treatise our system will guide the user through the relevant legal material (authoritative quotes, relevant argumentation and precedents). The system will help the user to spot the difficult issues and can also supply related hypothetical cases.

JURIX is actually a domain-independent shell. At present a knowledge-base has been established for Common-Law Nuisance.

Research Problem Seven: A **JURIX**-like system may be implemented in any area of law exhibiting the same kind of structure. It should be interesting to check for which legal domains this is possible. Furthermore, it may be possible to apply the concept-driven approach in other areas outside the legal domain, where decisions also depend on human discretionary judgment.

No other area where case-based reasoning takes place has been classified by authorities like case-law. This raises the question how to approach the building of **JURIX**-

like systems. We shall discuss this below, in research problem thirteen.

Concerning our second system, Meta, it is clear how it could be implemented in other areas with respect to a specific problem, e.g. the 'hard to heat' problem. This would of course assume that the necessary information about previous cases and their decisions was made available.

Research Problem Eight: Each application area usually deals with several questions of the 'hard to heat' type. Is it necessary to build a separate Meta-like system for each question, or is it possible to incorporate several such systems into one comprehensive system. If such a process is found to be possible, it may be a step towards applying the same approach in general legal areas.

4. Evaluation of JURIX and Meta.

The approach to legal reasoning as implemented in **JURIX** is undoubtly used by legal practitioners. However, it is not the only possible one. The HYPO system, for example, uses a slightly different approach in considering a case according to the so called dimensions.

Research Problem Nine: It could be interesting to combine the two approaches exhibited in HYPO and **JURIX**. There are also other ways of approaching legal reasoning and analysis. They should also be examined from the point of view of a unified computer implementation.

The problems we have discussed which are related to the use of analogy have no solution in **JURIX**. However, as it needs no common-sense knowledge it can be applied to any case in the particular area of law where it is implemented.

At present **JURIX** simply retrieves relevant cases and organizes them for the user. However, no weighing of these cases take place. As we have seen in section 3.4.3.5 the HYPO system makes a first step towards such weighing.

Research Problem Ten: It seems important to support the user in such a weighing process. If many precedents have been retrieved the system ought to be able to present them in some order of importance and help the user narrow down the choice of important issues of the case at hand. The method of weighing in Meta is only one step in this direction.

We have shown a prototype of **JURIX** to a practicing barrister who is an expert on nuisance-cases. He tested the system by supplying some actual and hypothetical cases. In one of them **JURIX** retrieved an argument he had not thought of himself. We have also considered some lawyer's opinions. In England such an opinion is produced by a specialist for a general practitioner who has a case in the particular area of law. For reasons of confidentiality they cannot be reproduced here, however, we can briefly explain what they look like. They spot issues of the case at hand which may be problematic, pointing to precedents just like Salmond - and **JURIX** - do. If the case at hand should proceed more detail would be produced and experiential matters would be considered. Our attempts at evaluating **JURIX** raises the following problem:

Research Problem Eleven: Assuming that computer systems for case-law will be developed on a more extensive scale in the future. How does one evaluate the power of such a system and its practical applicability, and how does one compare two such systems to each other.

The Meta system has been in practical use in our department. The main problem seems to be the number of precedents and arguments that are retrieved. It seems to be too large for the advisors to comfortably survey during an interactive session. Some of the rules used to tune the system, i.e. to cut down the number of retrieved cases have been ad hoc.

Research Problem Twelve: The approach to legal reasoning through meta-rules looks promising. However, while a human seems able to prune the supply of somewhat relevant precedents in an efficient manner, Meta does that only with difficulty.

5. Rule Generation.

The top-down approach pre-supposes the existence of an authoritative treatise from which the implementator can construct a set of rules. Such a text-book may not always be available, for several reasons:

(1) An existing treatise has become obsolete.
(2) No treatise was ever written in the particular area of law.
(3) The area of law may be an area of new legislation which gives rise to subsequent new case-law.

Research problem Thirteen: It may be worthwhile to build a component to precede the present part of **JURIX** for establishing general rules based on case-law. In other words, we propose the development of a program which can support a human expert in creating a Salmond-like work, but directly in the form of a set of logical implications. In other areas of case-based reasoning there is a complete lack of Salmond-like treatises. The research problem may therefore be generalized as follows:

Research Problem Fourteen: In any given area of case-based reasoning to develop a computer program for creating (and updating) a set of logic rules used as indices to the given case-base.

6. Paradigms.

All the works and systems described in this book have used either a rule-based or a case-based approach. It appears that both have their place within the framework of legal computer systems.

We have not considered the very small number of papers relating to yet another paradigm: Connectionism or Neural Networks. In the legal domain this approach has been applied in: [Fernhout89], [Bochereau91] and [Rose89]. The latter paper deals with classical information retrieval. Two additional papers on neural nets address problems of open texture: [Philipps89] and [vanOpdorp91].

Research problem Fifteen: Systems based on neural nets lack transparency and have little or no explanatory facilities. Is it nevertheless possible to apply this paradigm in areas where other approaches have not yet succeeded. Such application could be in isolated systems or as components in hybrid systems.

The main aim of this book has been to put the problems of case-law computer systems in the proper perspective. We have done this by critically examining previous systems and related work and by developing two system which take different, but not necessarily more advanced approaches to the problem. These approaches are, however, practical in the sense that applicable computer systems may be developed with the present state-of-the-art. Nevertheless, as illustrated by the research problems suggested above, research in this area is only at its beginning and it has much challenging work to offer.

Appendix One

As explained in chapter five we have used the authoritative book by Salmond ([Salmond81]) to extract a set of rules of logic expressing necessary and sufficient conditions for nuisance. These rules form the basis from which the and-or tree is constructed and are stated below.

nuisance   **if**   appropriate-length-of-time
             and   appropriate-situation-of-plaintiffs-premises
             and   impaired-use-or-enjoyment-of-plaintiffs-premises
             and   sensible-damage
             and   no-extraordinary-or-sensitive-use-of-plaintiffs-premises
             and   competent-plaintiff
             and   liable-defendant
             and   unacceptable-excuse
             and   defendant-has-responsibility
             and   defendant-has-no-defence

appropriate-length-of-time
             if   action-is-continuous
             or   action-is-repetitive
             or   action-was-for-short-time-only
             or   action-is-intermittent
             or   action-happened-on-few-occasions-only
             or   action-happened-on-one-occasion only

appropriate-situation-of-plaintiffs-premises
        if   plaintiffs-premises-neighbour-premises-of-activity

impaired-use-or-enjoyment-of-plaintiffs-premises
        if   physical-damages-to-plaintiffs-premises
        or   prevention-of-use-or-enjoyment-by-discomfort-to-plaintiff
        or   injury-to-servitude

injury-to-servitude
        if   injury-to-rights-of-way
        or   injury-to-rights-of-entry-to-dominant-land
        or   injury-to-rights-of-support
        or   injury-to-rights-of-light-and-air
        or   injury-to-rights-of-water
        or   injury-to-rights-of-nuisance-acts-on-servient-land
        or   injury-to-rights-of-placing-and-keeping-things-on-servient
        or   injury-to-profit-a-prendre
        or   not-injury-to-uninterupted-view
        or   not-injury-to-right-of-privacy

sensible-damage
        if   appreciable-injury-to-premises
        or   appreciable-relative-discomfort-to-plaintiff
        or   appreciable-disturbance-of-servitude

competent-plaintiff
        if   plaintiff-is-owner-occupier-of-premises
        or   plaintiff-is-tenant-of-premises
        or   plaintiff-is-revisioner
                 and
                 permanent-injury-to-proprietary-rights
        or   plaintiff-is-licensee
                 and
                 plaintiff-has-exclusive-possession-of-premises
        or   plaintiff-is-member-of-occupiers-family
                 and
                 plaintiff-resides-on-premises
        or   plaintiff-has-de-facto-possession
        or   intent-to-recover-damages-from-before-acquisition

liable-defendant
        if   owner-occupier-of-premises-where-nuisance-occurs
        or   lessee-of-premises-where-nuisance-occurs
        or   defendant-is-lessor-of-premises
                and
                lessee-does-not-act-in-nuisance
        or   defendant-is-lessor-of-premises
                and
                defendant-controls-part-of-premises-where-nuisance
        or   defendant-is-lessor-of-premises
                and
                burden-of-repair-is-undetermined
                and
                lessor-has-right-of-entry-to-premises
        or   defendant-is-lessor-of-premises
                and
                nuisance-due-to-disrepair
                and
                burden-of-repair-on-lessee
                and
                extremely-large-amount-of-work-needed
        or   defendant-is-licensor-of-premises
                and
                licensee-has-not-control-over-part-where-nuisance
        or   defendant-is-licensee-of-premises
                and
                licensee-has-control-over-part-where-nuisance
        or   defendant-is-authorizer-of-tortuous-act
                and
                defendant-has-involvment-in-action
        or   defendant-is-independant-contractor

defendant-has-involvment-in-action
        if   defendant-can-foresee-nuisance
        or   defendant-directed-act-of-nuisance
        or   defendant-has-control-of-act-of-nuisance
        or   defendant-is-responsible-for creation-of-nuisance

unacceptable-excuse
      if   plaintiff-came-to-nuisance
      or   plaintiff-contributed-to-action
      or   nuisance-beneficial-to-public-at-large
      or   all-possible-care-applied-to-prevent-nuisance
      and   action-not-authorized-by-statute
      or   joint-creation-of-nuisance
      and   each-contribution-too-small-to-be-nuisance
      or   injury-to-servitude
      and   plaintiff-has-de-facto-possession
      and   defendant-is-not-servient-owner
      and   defendant-claims-jus-tertii-of-dominant-owner
      or   injury-to-servitude
      and   plaintiff-has-de-facto-possession
      and   defendant-is-servient-owner
      and   service-is-natural
      and   defendant-claims-jus-tertii-of-dominant-owner

defendant-has-responsibility
      if   nuisance-due-to-other-factors
      and   defendant-adopts-continues-nuisance
      or   nuisance-not-taken-over-when-premises-acquired
      or   nuisance-not-due-to-latent-effect

nuisance-due-to-other-factors
      if   nuisance-due-to-act-of-strangers
      or   nuisance-due-to-act-of-trespasser
      or   nuisance-due-to-act--of-nature

defendant-adopts-continues-nuisance
      if   defendant-makes-use-of-nuisance
      or   defendant-knows-of-nuisance

defendant-has-no-defence
      if   state-of-affairs-is-not-ordinary
      or   activity-is-not-reasonably-undertaken
      or   right-not-acquired-by-prescription
      or   injury-to-servitude
              and
              plaintiff-has-de-facto-possession
              and
              defendant-is-servient-owner
              and
              defendant-claims-jus-tertii-of-dominant-owner
              and
              servitude-is-not-acquired
      or   injury-to-servitude
               and
              plaintiff-has-no-legal-right-to-servitude
              and
              de-facto-enjoyment-of-servitude-not-protected
              and
              defendant-not-owner-occupier-of-premises-where-nuisance

state-of-affairs-is-not-ordinary
      if   dangerous-state-of-affairs
      or   not-ordinary-with-respect-to-locality
      or   state-not-widespread-and-general
      or   state-not-brought-on-by-nature

action-not-reasonably-undertaken
      if   means-of-proceeding-are-not-usual-or-expected
              and
              defendant-is-malicious
      or   proceedings-undertaken-with-skill-and-care
              and
              defendant-is-malicious
      or   expense-of-prevention-is-not-an-intolerable-burden

rights-not-acquired-by-prescription

	if	action-is-not-openly
	or	action-was-not-known-to-servient-tenent-owner
	or	action-not-caused-continuously-for-twenty-years
	or	harm-not-actionable-for-active-period

Appendix Two

The following table contains all legal computer systems mentioned in the text of this book. The section indicated is the one which contains the most information concerning the system. The year given is the one when a publication describing the system appeared.

Author	Name	Section	Year	Domain
Ashley et al.	HYPO	3.4.3	1987	Trade Secrets Law
Bellairs	BRAMBLE	4.4.5	1989	Corporate Acqusitions
Branting	GREBE	3.4.4.2	1989	Worker's Compensation Law
Capper et al.		1.4	1988	Latent Damage Act 1986
Gardner		3.4.2	1984	Contracts: Offer and Acceptance
Gelbart et al.	Flexicon	3.3.4.3	1991	
Greenleaf	DataLex	3.3.4.2.2	1987	
Goldman	STARE	3.3.3	1987	Contract Law
Hafner	LIRS	3.3.4.3	1978	U.S. Commercial Code
Hellawell	CORPTAX	4.3.2	1980	U.S.Tax Law
Meldman		3.4.1	1975	Assault and Battery
Mendelson		4.3.3	1989	Criminal Case Appeal
Michaelsen	TAXADVISOR	1.4	1982	U.S. Tax Law
McCarty	TAXMAN I	3.2.3	1977	U.S. Tax Law
Schild	**JURIX**	1.9	1988	Nuisance
Schild	Meta	1.10	1990	Student Regulations
Schlobohm		3.2.2.3	1985	U.S. Tax Law
Sergot et al.	BNA	3.2.2	1986	British Nationality Act
Skalak et al.	CABARET	3.4.4.1	1989	Statutory Interpretation
Vossos et al.	IKBALS II	3.4.4.2	1991	Statutory Interpretation
Waterman et al.	LDS	1.4	1980	Claims Adjustment

References

[Allen57]   Allen L.E.
               Symbolic Logic: A Razor-edged Tool for Drafting and Interpreting Legal
               Documents.
               Yale Law Journal, 66, 1957.

[Allen80]   Allen L.E.
               Language,Law and Logic. Plain Legal Drafting for the Electronic Age.
               in: Niblett B. (editor):
               Computer Science and Law.
               Cambridge University Press, Cambridge, 1980.

[Allen86]   Allen L.E., Saxon C.S.
               Analysis of the Logical Structure of Legal Rules by a Modernized and
               Formalized Version of Hohfeld's Fundamental Conceptions.
               in: Martino A.A., Socci Natali F. (editors):
               Automatic Analysis of Legal Texts.
               North-Holland, Amsterdam, 1986, p.385-450.

[Allen89]   Allen L.E., Saxon C.S.
               Relationship of Expert Systems to the Operation of a Legal System.
               III International Conference on Logica, Informatica, Diritto,
               Florence, 1989, Appendix, p.1-15.

[Allen91]   Allen L.E., Saxon C.S.
               More IA Needed in AI: Interpretation Assistance for Coping With the
               Problem of Multiple Structural Interpretations.
               Proc.Third Int. Conference on AI and Law, ACM Press, p.53-61, 1991.

[Ashley85]   Ashley K.D.
               Reasoning by Analogy: A Survey of Selected AI Research with
               Implications for Legal Expert Systems.
               in: Walter C. (editor):
               Computer Power and Legal Reasoning.
               West Publ.Co., St. Paul, 1985.

[Ashley87a]   Ashley K.D., Rissland E.L.
But, See, Accord: Generating "Blue Book"
Citations in HYPO.
Proc. First Int. Conf. on AI and Law, ACM Press,1987, p.67-74.

[Ashley87b]   Ashley K.D., Rissland E.L.
Compare and Contrast, A Test of Expertise.
Proc. of AAAI Conference, 1987.

[Ashley88]   Ashley K.D., Rissland E.L.
Waiting on Weighing: A Symbolic Least Commitment
Approach.
Proc. of AAAI Conference, 1988.

[Ashley89]   Ashley K.D.
Toward a Computational Theory of Arguing with Precedents.
Proc. Second Int. Conf. on AI and Law, ACM Press, 1989, p.93-102.

[Ashley90]   Ashley K.D.
Modeling Legal Argument.
Bradford Books/MIT Press, Boston, 1990.

[Bellairs89]   Bellairs K.
Contextual Relevance in Analogical Reasoning: A Model of Legal
Argument.
Ph.D. Thesis, University of Minnesota, 1989.

[Bench88]   Bench-Capon T., Sergot M.J.
Towards a Rule-Based Representation of Open Texture in Law.
in Walter C. (editor)
Computing Power and Legal Language.
Greenwood/Quorum Press, 1988, p.39-60.

[Bench89]   Bench-Capon T.
Deep Models, Normative Reasoning and Legal Expert Systems.
Proc. Second Int. Conf. on AI and Law, ACM Press, 1989.

[Bench91]   Bench-Capon T.
Exploiting Isomorphism: Development of a KBS to Support British Coal
Insurance Claims.
Proc. Third Int. Conf. on AI and Law, ACM Press, 1991, p.62-68.

[Bench91a]   Bench-Capon T., Coenen F.
Practical Application of KBS to Law: The Crucial Role of Maintenance.
in: van Noortwijk C., Schmidt A.H.J., Winkels R.F.G. (editors)
Knowledge Based Systems; Aims for research and Development.
Koninklijke Vermande Bv, The Netherlands, 1991, p.5-17.

[Bing80]   Bing J.
Legal Norms, Discretionary Rules and Computer Programs.
in: Niblett B. (editor)
Computer Science and Law.
Cambridge University Press, 1980, p.119-136.

[Bing87]   Bing J.
                   Performance of Legal Text Retrieval Systems.
                   Law Library Journal, vol. 79, 2, 1987.

[Bing89]   Bing J.
                   The Law of the Books and the Law of the Files.
                   in: Vandeberghe G.P.V. (editor)
                   Advanced Topics of Law and Information Technology.
                   Kluwer, 1989, p.151-182.

[Birnbaum80]   Birnbaum L., Flowers M., McGuire R.
                   Towards an AI Model of Argumentation.
                   Proc. AAAI, Morgan Kaufmann, 1980, p.313-315.

[Birnbaum82]   Birnbaum L.
                   Argument Molecules: A Functional Representation of Argument
                   Structure.
                   Proc. AAAI, Morgan Kaufmann, 1982, p.63-65.

[Bochereau91]   Bochereau L., Bourcier D., Bourgine P.
                   Extracting Legal Knowledge by Means of a Multilayer Neural Network.
                   Proc. Third Int. Conf. on AI and Law, ACM Press, 1991, p.288-295.

[Branting89]   Branting L.K.
                   Representing and Reusing Explanations of Legal Precedents.
                   Proc. Second Int. Conf. on AI and Law, ACM Press, 1989, p.103-110.

[Branting90]   Branting L.K.
                   Integrating Rules and Precedents for Classification and Explanations.
                   Ph.D. Thesis, AI Laboratory, University of Texas, TR AI90-146,
                   Austin, Texas, 1990.

[Branting91]   Branting L.K.
                   Reasoning with Portions of Precedents.
                   Proc. Int. Conf. on AI and Law, ACM Press, 1991, p.145-154.

[Bratley91]   Bratley P., Fremont J., Mackaay E., Poulin D.
                   Coping with Change.
                   Proc. Third Int. Conf. on AI and Law, ACM Press, 1991.

[Brody80]   Brody S.A.
                   The Post-Macomber Cases in Taxman II
                   Framework.
                   LRP-TR-5, Rutgers University, 1980

[Buckley81]   Buckley R.A.
                   The Law of Nuisance.
                   Butterworths, London,1981

[Capper88]   Capper P.N., Susskind R.
                   Latent Damage Law - The Expert System.
                   Butterworths, London, 1988.

[DARPA89]   Case-Based Reasoning.
               Proceedings of the DARPA Workshop on Case-Based Reasoning.
               Morgan-Kaufmann Publ., USA, 1989, p.1-13.

[Chandra83]   Chandrasekaran B., Mittal S.
               Deep versus Compiled Knowledge Approaches to
               Diagnostic Problem Solving.
               Int. J. Man-Machine Studies, 1983

[Charniak85]   Charniak E., McDermott D.
               Introduction to Artificial Intelligence.
               Addison-Wesley, Reading Mass.,1985

[Clark84]   Clark K.L., McCabe F.G.
               micro-Prolog: Programming in Logic.
               Prentice-Hall, 1984

[Clerk82]   Dias R.W.M. (General Editor).
               Clerk & Lindsell on Torts.
               15th ed., Sweet & Maxwell, London, 1982

[Cross77]   Cross R.
               Precedent in English Law.
               Oxford University Press, 1977.

[Dias84]   Dias R.W.M., Markesinis B.S.
               Tort Law.
               Oxford University Press, Oxford, 1984

[Duda80]   Duda R.O.
               The PROSPECTOR System for Mineral Exploration.
               SRI Project 8172, SRI International, 1980

[Dworkin67]   Dworkin R.
               The Model of Rules.
               University of Chicago Law Review, 35, 1967

[Dworkin75]   Dworkin R.
               Hard Cases.
               Harvard Law Review, 88, 1975.

[Dworkin77]   Dworkin R.
               Taking Rights Seriously.
               Duckworth, London, 1977.

[Dworkin85]   Dworkin R.
               A Matter of Principle.
               Harvard University Press, 1985.

[Dworkin86]   Dworkin R.
               Law's Empire.
               Fontana, London, 1986.

[Dyer85]   Dyer M.G., Flowers M.
                Toward Automating Legal Expertise.
                in: Walter C. (editor)
                Computing Power and Legal reasoning.
                West Publ. Co., St. Paul, 1985.

[Ellman89]   Ellman T.
                Explanation-Based Learning: A Survey of Programs and Perspectives.
                Computing Surveys, 21, 1989, p. 163.

[Ernst69]   Ernst G., Newell A.
                GPS: A Case Study in Generality and Problem Solving.
                Academic Press, New York, 1969.

[Fernhout89]   Fernhout F.
                Using a Parallel Distributed Processing Model as Part of a Legal Expert
                System.
                III International Conference on Logica, Informatica, Diritto,
                Florence, 1989, vol.1, p.255-268.

[Flowers82]   Flowers M., McGuire R., Birnbaum L.
                Adversary Arguments and the Logic of personal Attacks.
                in: Lehnert W., Rigle M. (editors)
                Strategies for Natural Language Processing.
                Lawrence Erlbaum Ass., Hillsdale, NJ, 1982.

[Frank49]   Frank J.J.
                Law and the Modern Mind.
                Brentano, New York, 2nd ed., 1949.

[Fuller58]   Fuller L.L.
                Harvard Law Review, 71, 1958, p.630-672.
                reprinted in:
                Olafson F.A. (editor):
                Society, Law and Morality.
                Prentice-Hall, Englewood Cliffs, N.J., 1961.

[Fuller72]   Fuller L.L., Eisenberg M.A.
                Basic Contract Law.
                3rd ed., West Publ. Co., St. Paul, 1972.

[Gardner84]   Gardner A.
                An Artificial Intelligence Approach to
                Legal Reasoning.
                STAN-CS-85-1045, Stanford University, 1984.

[Gardner87]   Gardner A.
                An Artificial Intelligence Approach to
                Legal Reasoning.
                Bradford Books/ MIT Press, Boston, 1987.

[Gelbart91]   Gelbart D., Smith J.C.
                Beyond Boolean Search: FLEXICON, A Legal Text-Based Intelligent
                System.

Proc. Third Int. Conf. AI and Law, ACM Press, 1991, p.225-234.

[Genesereth84]   Genesereth M.R., Greiner R., Smith D.E.
MRS Manual.
Memo HPP-80-24, Stanford Heuristic Programming Project.
Stanford University, 1980, revised 1984.

[Gilburne82]   Gilburne M.R., Johnston R.L.
Trade Secret Protection for Software Generally and in
the Mass Market.
Computer/Law Journal III(3), 1982.

[Goldman87]   Goldman S.R., Dyer M.G., Flowers M.
Precedent-Based Legal Reasoning and Knowledge
Acquisition in Contract Law: A Process Model.
Proc. First Int. Conf. on AI and Law, ACM Press, 1987, p.210.

[Greenleaf87]   Greenleaf G., Mowbray A., Tyree A.L.
Expert Systems in Law: The Datalex Project.
Proc. First Int. Conf. on AI and Law, ACM Press, 1987, p.9.

[[Goguen83]   Goguen J.A., Weiner J.L., Linde C.
Reasoning and Natural Explanation.
Int. J. Man-Machine Studies, 19, 1983.

[Hafner78]   Hafner C.D.
An Information Retrieval System Based on a Conceptual
Model of Legal Knowledge.
Ph.D. Thesis, University of Michigan, 1978.

[Hafner81]   Hafner C.D.
An Information Retrieval System based on a Conceptual
Model of Legal Knowledge.
UMI Research Press, Ann Arbor, 1981.

[Hafner87]   Hafner C.D.
Conceptual Organization of Case Law
Knowledge Bases.
Proc. First Int. Conf. on AI and Law, ACM Press,1987, p.35.

[Hall89]   Hall R.P.
Computational Approaches to Analogical Reasoning: A Comparative
Analysis.
Artificial Intelligence, 39, 1989, p.39-120.

[Hammond83]   Hammond P., Sergot M.J.
A Prolog Shell for Logic Based Expert Systems.
Proc. 3rd BCS Expert Systems Conference, 1983.

[Hammond83a]   Hammond P., Sergot M.J.
Logic for representing Data and Expertise.
Imperial College, London, 1983.

[Hammond84]   Hammond P., Sergot M.J.
               APES Reference Manual.
               Logic Based Systems, London, 1984.

[Hart58]   Hart H.L.A.
               Positivism and the Separation of Law and Morals.
               Harvard Law Review, 71, 1958.

[Hart61]   Hart H.L.A.
               The Concept of Law.
               Oxford University Press, Oxford, 1961.

[Hart83]   Hart H.L.A.
               Problems of the Philosophy of Law.
               in: Hart H.L.A.
               Essays in Jurisprudence and Philosophy.
               Oxford University Press, Oxford, 1983.

[Hart82]   Hart P. E.
               Directions for AI in the Eighties.
               SIGART Newsletter, 79, 1982.

[Hart86]   Hart P.E.
               Artificial Intelligence in Transition.
               in: Kowalik J.S. (editor)
               Knowledge based Problem Solving.
               Prentice-Hall, 1986, p.296-310.

[Hayes-Roth83] Hayes-Roth F., Waterman D.A., Lenat D.B.
               Building Expert Systems.
               Addison-Wesley, Reading Mass., 1983.

[Hayes-Roth84] Hayes-Roth F.
               Knowledge-Based Expert Systems.
               Computer, vol.17, 1984.

[Hellawell80] Hellawell R.
               A Computer Program for Legal Planning and
               Analysis: Taxation and Stock Redemptions.
               Columbia Law Review, 80, 1980.

[Hilpinen71]   Hilpinen R.
               Deontic Logic: Introductory and Systematic Readings.
               Reidel Publ., Dordrecht, 1971.

[Hohfeld13]   Hohfeld W.N.
               Some Fundamental Legal Conceptions as Applied in Judicial
               Reasoning.
               Yale Law Journal, 23, 1913, p.16.

[Hohfeld17]   Hohfeld W.N.
               Fundamental Legal Conceptions as Applied in Judicial
               Reasoning.
               Yale Law Journal, 27, 1917, p.710.

[Hohfeld19]   Hohfeld W. N.
                Fundamental Concepts as Applied in Judicial Reasoning.
                Yale University Press, New Haven, 1919.
                This paper is actually a joint publication of the two previous papers:
                [Hohfeld13] and [Hohfeld17].

[Hustler82]   Hustler A.
                Programming Law in Logic.
                Report CS-82-13, Dept. of Computer Science,
                University of Waterloo, Canada, 1982.

[Kanger71]   Kanger S.
                New Foundations for Ethical Theory.
                in: Hilpinen R.
                Deontic Logic: Introductory and Systematic Readings.
                Reidel Publ., Dordrecht, 1971, p.36-58.

[Kass90]   Kass J.M.
                Developing Creative Hypotheses by Adapting Explanations.
                Ph.D. Thesis, Yale University, 1990.
                also published as:
                Northwestern University, Institute for the Learning Sciences,
                Technical Report #6, November, 1990.

[Kauffman87]   Kauffman S.B.
                Electronic Databases in Legal Research.
                Rutgers Computer and Technology Law J., 1987.

[Kedar84]   Kedar-Cabelli S.
                Analogy with Purpose in Legal Reasoning from Precedents.
                LRP-TR-17, Rutgers University, 1984.

[King76]   King J.J.
                Analysis of KRL Implementation of a Current Legal
                Reasoning Program Design.
                Unpublished, May, 1976.

[Klein87]   Klein D., Finin T.
                What's in a Deep Model?
                Proceedings of IJCAI 1987.

[Knight90]   Knight K.
                Connectionist Ideas and Algorithms.
                CACM, vol.33, 1990, p.59-74.

[Kolodner91]   Kolodner J.L.
                Improving Human Decision Making through Case-Based Decision
                Aiding.
                AI Magazine, vol. 12, 2, Summer 1991, p. 52-68.

[Kowalski79]   Kowalski R.A.
                Logic for Problem Solving.
                North-Holland, Amsterdam, 1979.

[Lawlor80]   Lawlor R.C.
Computer Analysis of Judicial Decisions.
in: Niblett B. (editor)
Computer Science and Law.
Cambridge University Press, Cambridge, 1980.

[Lenat90]   Lenat D.B., Ramanthan V.G., Pittman K., Pratt D., Shepperd M.
CYC: Towards Programs with Common Sense.
CACM, vol.33, no. 8, p.30-49.

[Llewellyn51]   Llewellyn K.N.
The Bramble Bush.
Oceana Publ., New York, 1951.

[Llewellyn60]   Llewellyn K.N.
The Common Law Tradition: Deciding Appeals.
Little, Brown, Boston 1960.

[Loevinger49]   Loevinger L.
Jurimetrics: The Next Step Forward.
Minn. L. Rev., 33, 1949, p.455.

[Loevinger61]   Loevinger L.
Jurimetrics: Science and Prediction in the Field of Law.
Minnesota Law Review, 46, 1961, p.255.

[Lowerre80]   Lowerre B., Reddy R.
The HARPY Speech Understanding System.
in: Lea W. (editors)
Trends in Speech Recognition.
Prentice Hall, 1980.

[Marshall89]   Marshall C.C.
Representing the Structure of a Legal Argument.
Proc. Second Int. Conf. on AI and Law, ACM Press, 1989.

[McCarty77]   McCarty L.T.
Reflections on Taxman: An Experiment in AI and Legal Reasoning.
Harvard Law Review, 90, 1977

[McCarty80]   McCarty L.T.
The Taxman Project.
in: Niblett B. (editor)
Computer Science and Law.
Cambridge University Press, Cambridge, 1980

[McCarty80a]   McCarty L.T.
Some Requirements for a Computer-Based Legal Consultant.
LRP-TR-8, Rutgers University, 1980

[McCarty82]   McCarty L.T., Sridharan N.S.
A Computational Theory of Legal Argument.
LRP-TR-13, Rutgers University, 1982

[McCarty82a]   McCarty L.T.
                 A Computational Theory of Eisner v. Macomber.
                 in: Ciampi C. (editor)
                 AI and Legal Information Systems.
                 North Holland, Amsterdam, 1982

[McCarty83]   McCarty L.T.
                 Permissions and Obligations.
                 Proceedings of IJCAI, 1983

[McCarty83a]   McCarty L.T.
                 Intelligent Legal Information Systems:
                 Problems and Prospects.
                 Rutgers Computers and Tech. Law Journal, 1983

[McCarty86]   McCarty L.T.
                 Permissions and Obligations: An Informal
                 Introduction.
                 in: Martino A.A., Socci Natali F. (editors)
                 Automated Analysis of Legal Texts.
                 North Holland, Amsterdam, 1986.

[McCarty89]   McCarty L.T.
                 Computing with Prototypes.
                 Bar Ilan Symposium on the Foundations of AI, 1989.

[McCarty89a]   McCarty L.T.
                 A Language for Legal Discourse.
                 Proc. Second Int. Conf. on AI and Law, ACM Press, 1989.

[McCarty91]   McCarty L.T.
                 On the Role of Prototypes in Appellate Legal Argument.
                 Proc. Third Int. Conf. on AI and Law, ACM Press, 1991, p.185-190.

[McCarty91a]   McCarty L.T., van der Meyden R.
                 Indefinite Reasoning with Definite Rules.
                 Proc. Twelfth Int. Joint Conf. on AI, 1991.

[McCarty91b]   McCarty L.T.
                 Circumscribing Embedded Implications.
                 Proc. First Int. Workshop on Logic programming and Non-Monotonic
                 Reasoning, MIT Press, Boston, 1991.

[McGuire81]   McGuire R., Birnbaum L., Flowers M.
                 Opportunistic Processing in Arguments.
                 Proc. IJCAI, Morgan Kaufmann, 1981, p.58-60.

[Meldman75]   Meldman J.A.
                 A Preliminary Study in Computer-Aided Legal Analysis.
                 Technical Report, MAC-TR-157, M.I.T., 1975

[Mendelson89]   Mendelson S.
                 An Attempted Dimensional Analysis of the Law Governing

Government Appeals in Criminal Cases.
Proc. Second Int. Conf. on AI and Law, ACM Press, 1989.

[Merkl90]   Merkl W., Vieweg S., Karapetjan A.
KELP: A Hypertext Oriented User Interface for an Intelligent
Legal Fulltext Information Retrieval System.
Proc. DEXA-90, Vienna, 1990.

[Merryman85]   Merryman J.H.
The Civil Law Tradition.
Stanford University Press, 2ed., 1985.

[Michaelsen82] Michaelsen R.H.
A Knowledge Based System for Individual Income and Transfer Tax
Planning.
Ph.D. Thesis, University of Illinois, 1982.

[Michaelsen84] Michaelsen R.H.
An Expert System for Federal Tax Planning.
Expert Systems, vol.1, 2, 1984.

[Mitchell86]   Mitchell T.M., Keller R.M., Kedar-Cabelli S.T.
Explanation-Based Generalization: A Unifying View.
Machine Learning 1, 1986, p.47-80.

[Nagel87]   Nagel D.J.
Learning Concepts with a Prototype Based Model for
Concept Representation.
Ph.D. Thesis, Rutgers University, 1987.

[Negoita85]   Negoita C.V.
Expert Systems and Fuzzy Systems.
Benjamin/Cummings, Menlo Park, 1985.

[Nilsson80]   Nilsson N.I.
Principles of Artificial Intelligence.
Tioga Press, Palo Alto, 1980.

[Perelman63]   Perelman C.
The Idea of Justice and the Problem of Argument.
Routledge and Kegan Paul, London, 1963.

[Perelman69]   Perelman C., Olbrechts-Tyteca L.
The New Rhetoric: A Treatise on Argumentation.
University of Notre dame Press, 1969.

[Perelman82]   Perelman C.
The Realm of Rhetoric.
University of Notre dame Press, 1982.

[Philipps89]   Philipps L.
Are Legal Decisions Based on the Application of Rules or Prototype
Recognition?

III International Conference on Logica, Informatica, Diritto, Florence, 1989, vol.2, p.673-680

[Phillips60]   Phillips H.B.
Felix Frankfurter Reminiscences.
Secker and Warburg, London, 1960, p.98-101.

[Prosser41]   Prosser W.L.
Handbook of the Law of Torts.
West Publ., St. Paul, 1941.
(This old edition is the one referenced by Meldman, even though the 4th ed. was published in 1972).

[Reddy76]   Reddy R., Erman L., Fennell R., Neely R.
The HEARSAY Speech Understanding System.
IEEE Trans. Computers, 1976.

[Reichman84]   Reichman-Adar R.
Extended Person-Machine Interface.
Artificial Intelligence, vol.22, 1984, p.157-218.

[Reisinger82]   Reisinger L.
Legal Reasoning by Analogy. A Model applying Fuzzy Set Theory.
in: Ciampi C. (editor)
AI and Legal Information Systems.
North Holland, Amsterdam, 1982, p.151.

[Restatement81]   Restatement of the Law, Second: Contracts 2d.
American Law Institute Publ., St. Paul, 3 vols., 1981.

[Rissland87]   Rissland E.L., Ashley K.D.
A Case-Based System for Trade Secrets Law.
Proc. First Int. Conf. on AI and Law, ACM Press,1987, p.61-66.

[Rissland89]   Rissland E.L., Skalak D.B.
Interpreting Statutory Predicates.
Proc. Second Int. Conf. on AI and Law, ACM Press, 1989, p.46-53.

[Rissland 89a]   Rissland E.L., Skalak D.B.
Combining Case-Based and Rule-Based Reasoning.
Proc. Eleventh Int. Joint Conf. on Artificial Intelligence, Detroit, 1989.

[Rose89]   Rose D.E., Below R.K.
Legal Information Retrieval: A Hybrid Approach.
Proc. Second Int. Conf. on AI and Law, ACM Press, 1989, p.138-146.

[Salmond81]   Heuring R.F.V., Chambers R.S.
Salmond and Heuring on the Law of Torts.
18th ed., Sweet and Maxwell, London, 1981.

[Salmond87]   Heuring R.F.V., Buckley R.A.
Salmond and Heuring on the Law of Torts.
19th ed., Sweet and Maxwell, London, 1987.

[Salton83]   Salton G., McGill M.J.
                Introduction to Modern Information Retrieval.
                McGraw Hill, New York, 1983.

[Schank74]   Schank R., Rieger C.J.
                Inference and the Computer Understanding of natural Language.
                Artificial Intelligence, vol. 5, 4, 1974, p.373-412.

[Schild88]   Schild U.J.
                JURIX: A Legal Expert System.
                8th Int. Workshop on Expert Systems, Avignon, 1988.

[Schild89]   Open Texture and Case-Law Computer Systems.
                III International Conference on Logica, Informatica, Diritto,
                Florence, 1989, vol.1, p.623-641

[Schild90]   Schild U.J.
                Expert Systems, Meta-Rules and Quasi-Legal Domains.
                10th Int. Workshop on Expert Systems, Avignon, 1990.

[Schlobohm85]   Schlobohm D.A.
                A Prolog Program Which Analyzes Income Tax Issues Under
                Section 318(a) of the Internal Revenue Code.
                in: Walter C. (editor)
                Computing Power and Legal Reasoning.
                West Publ., St. Paul, 1985, p.765-815.

[Sergot82]   Sergot M.J.
                Prospects for Representing the Law as Logic programs.
                in: Clark K., Taernlund S.-A. (editors):
                Logic Programming.
                Academic Press, 1982.

[Sergot83]   Sergot M.J.
                Query-the-user Facility for Logic Programming.
                in: Degano P., Sandewall E. (editors)
                Proc.Europ. Conf. on Integrated Interactive Systems.
                North Holland, Amsterdam, 1983.

[Sergot86]   Sergot M.J.
                Representing Legislation as Logic Programs.
                Machine Intelligence 11, 1986.

[Sergot86a]   Sergot M.J. et al.
                The British Nationality Act as Logic Programs.
                CACM, 29, 1986.

[Sergot91]   Sergot M.J.
                The Representation of Law in Computer Programs:
                in: Bench-Capon T. (editor)
                Knowledge-based Systems and Legal Applications.
                Academic Press, 1991, p.3-67.

[Shortliffe76] Shortliffe E.H.

Computer-based Medical Consultation: MYCIN.
American Elsevier, New York, 1976.

[Skalak91]   Skalak D.B., Rissland E.L.
               Argument Moves in a Rule-Guided Domain.
               Proc. Third Int. Conf. on AI and Law, ACM Press, 1991, p.1-11.

[Slade91]   Slade S.
               Case-Based reasoning: A Research Paradigm.
               AI Magazine, vol. 12, 1, Spring 1991, p.42-55.

[Sridharan78] Sridharan N.S.
               AIMDS User Manual, Version 2.
               CBM-TR-89, Rutgers University, 1978.

[Steels86]   Steels L.
               Learning in Second Generation Expert Systems.
               in: Kowalik J.S. (editor)
               Knowledge Based Problem Solving.
               Prentice-Hall, 1986, p.296-310.

[Steels89]   Steels L.
               The Deepening of Expert Systems.
               in: Campbell J., Cuena J. (editors)
               Perspectives of AI, vol. I, Halstead Press, NewYork, 1989, p.17-29.

[Susskind87]   Susskind R.
               Expert Systems in Law.
               Oxford University Press, Oxford, 1987.

[Susskind89]   Susskind R.
               The Latent Damage System: A Jurisprudential Analysis.
               Proc. Second Int. Conf. on AI and Law, ACM Press, 1989, p. 23 -32.

[Susskind89a] Susskind R., Capper P.
               The Latent Damage System - A First Generation Expert System in Law.
               III International Conference on Logica, Informatica, Diritto,
               Florence, 1989, vol.1, p.595-606.

[Sussman71]   Sussman G., Charniak E., Winograd T.
               Micro-planner Reference Manual.
               AI-203A, MIT-AI-Laboratory, 1971.

[Szolovits77] Szolovits P., Hawkinson L.B., Martin W.A.
               An Overview of OWL, a Language for
               Knowledge Representation.
               MIT/ LCS/ TM-86, 1977.

[Tapper80]   Tapper C.
               Citations as a Tool for Searching Law by Computer.
               in: Niblett B. (editor)
               Computer Science and Law.
               Cambridge University Press, Cambridge, 1980.

[Thorne80]   Thorne J.F. III
                Mathematics, Fuzzy Negligence and The Logic of Res Ipsa Loquitur.
                Northwestern University Law Review, 75, 1980.
                Reprinted in: Jurimetrics, 22, 1981, p.92.

[Toulmin72]   Toulmin S.
                Human Understanding: The Collective Use and Evolution of Concepts.
                Princeton University Press, 1972.

[Toulmin79]   Toulmin S., Rieke R.D., Janik A.
                An Introduction to Reasoning.
                MacMillan Press, New York, 1979.

[Twining74]   Twining W.L.
                British Journal of Law and Society, 148 (1949) at p.154.

[vanOpdorp91]   van Opdorp G.J., Walker R.F., Schrickx J.A., Groendijk C,
                van den Berg P.H.
                Networks at Work.
                Third Int. Conf. on AI and Law, ACM Press, 1991, p.278-287.

[vonMehren77]   vonMehren A.T., Gardly J.R.
                The Civil Law System.
                Little, Brown & Co., 2ed., New York, 1977.

[vonWright51]   vonWright G.H.
                Deontic Logic.
                Mind, 60, 1951, p.1-15.

[vonWright63]   von Wright G. H.
                Norm and Action.
                Humanities Press, New York, 1963.

[Vossos91]   Vossos G., Zeleznikow J., Dillon T., Vossos V.
                An Example of Integrating Legal Case-based reasoning with Object
                Oriented Rule-Based Systems: IKBALS II.
                Proc. Third Int. Conf. on AI and Law, ACM Press, 1991, p.31-41.

[Waismann45]   Waismann F.
                Verifiability.
                Proc. Aristotelian Soc., 19, 1945, p.119-150.
                reprinted in: Flew A. (editor)
                Logic and Language: First and Second Series,
                Anchor Books, Garden City, 1965, p.122-151.

[Waterman80]   Waterman D.E., Peterson M.A.
                Rule-Based Models of Legal Expertise.
                Proc. National Conf. on Artificial Intelligence.
                Stanford University, 1980.

[Waterman81]   Waterman D.E.
                Models of Legal Decision Making.
                Report R-2717-ICJ, Institute for Civil Justice,

The Rand Corporation, Santa Monica, Calif., 1981.

[Weir80]   Weir A.
               A Casebook on Tort.
               5th ed, Sweet and Maxwell, London, 1980.

[Weiss78]   Weiss S., Kulikowski C., Amarel S., Safir A.
               A Model-Based Method for Computer-Aided Medical Decision-Making.
               Artificial Intelligence, 11, 1978.

[Wellbank83]   Wellbank M.
               A Review of Knowledge Acquisition Techniques for Expert
               Systems.
               British Telecom, Ipswich, 1983.

[Winfield84]   Rogers W.V.H.
               Winfield and Jolowicz on Tort.
               Sweet & Maxwell, London, 1984.

[Winston82]   Winston P.H.
               Learning new Principles from Precedents and Exercises.
               Artificial Intelligence, 19, 1982, p.321-350.

[Winston84]   Winston P.H.
               Artificial Intelligence.
               Addison-Wesley, Reading Mass., 1984.

[Zadeh75]   Zadeh L.
               Fuzzy Logic and Approximate Reasoning.
               Synthese, 30, 1975.

The following is a list of books containing papers referenced above:

[Bench91a]   Bench-Capon T. (editor)
               Knowledge-based Systems and legal Applications.
               Academic Press, 1991, p.3-67.

[Campbell89]   Campbell J., Cuena J. (editors)
               Perspectives of AI, vol. I, Halstead Press, NewYork, 1989, p.17-29.

[Ciampi82]   Ciampi C. (editor)
               AI and Legal Information Systems.
               North Holland, Amsterdam, 1982.

[Clark82]   Clark K., Taernlund S.-A. (editors.):
               Logic Programming.
               Academic Press, 1982.

[Degano83]   Degano P., Sandewall E. (editors.)
               Proc.Europ. Conf. on Integrated Interactive Systems.
               North Holland, Amsterdam, 1983.

[Flew65]   Flew A. (editor)
                Logic and Language: First and Second Series,
                Anchor Books, Garden City, 1965, p.122-151.

[Hilpinen71]   Hilpinen R.
                Deontic Logic: Introductory and Systematic Readings.
                Reidel Publ., Dordrecht, 1971, p.36-58.

[Kowalik86]   Kowalik J.S. (editor)
                Knowledge based Problem Solving.
                Prentice-Hall, 1986, p.296-310.

[Lea80]   Lea W. (ed.)
                Trends in Speech Recognition.
                Prentice Hall, 1980.

[Lehnert82]   Lehnert W., Rigle M. (editors)
                Strategies for Natural language Processing.
                Lawrence Erlbaum Ass., Hillsdale, NJ, 1982.

[Martino86]   Martino A.A., Socci Natali F. (editors)
                Automated Analysis of Legal Texts.
                North Holland, Amsterdam, 1986.

[Niblett80]   Niblett B. (editor)
                Computer Science and Law.
                Cambridge University Press, 1980.

[Olafson61]   Olafson F.A. (editor):
                Society, Law and Morality.
                Prentice-Hall, Englewood Cliffs, N.J., 1961.

[Vandeberghe89] Vandeberghe G.P.V. (editor)
                Advanced Topics of Law and Information Technology.
                Kluwer, 1989, p.151-182.

[vanNoortwijk91] van Noortwijk C., Schmidt A.H.J., Winkels R.F.G. (editors)
                Knowledge Based Systems; Aims for Research and Development.
                Koninklijke Vermande Bv, The Netherlands, 1991.

[Walter85]   Walter C. (editor):
                Computer Power and Legal Reasoning.
                West Publ.Co., St. Paul, 1985.

[Walter88]   Walter C. (editor)
                Computing Power and Legal Language.
                Greenwood/Quorum Press, 1988.

Name Index

90, 95-99, 101-106, 108, 119, 122, 128, 129,
133, 136, 137, 140, 143-145, 160, 170, 184,
186-188, 190, 192-196
Artificial Intelligence, 19, 68, 121, 122, 157,
193
Assault and Battery, 82-86, 88, 114, 120, 141,
170, 187
AXEMAN, 71, 109, 137

Subject Index

Battery, *See* Assault and Battery
BRAMBLE, 145
British Nationality Act (BNA), 20, 62-66, 75,
87, 116, 122, 125, 127, 134, 146, 162

Academic Computer System,
15, 28, 30, 32, 44-49, 50, 56, 57, 61, 62, 74,
76, 79, 82, 109, 124, 126, 132, 137-140,
155, 157, 168, 192
Acceptance, *See* Contracts
Adjudicating Clerk, 18, 19, 26, 39, 141, 142,
143, 160, 172, 186, 190
AIMDS, 70, 100, 102, 104
Ambiguity, 14, 15, 17, 18, 28, 67, 68
    structural, 67,68
American Realists, 50
Analogy, 32, 52, 82, 83, 85, 86, 112, 121,
128, 129, 130, 134, 144-146, 184, 187, 189,
193, 195
Anglo-American Legal System, *See* Legal
Systems
Antecedent, 158, 166, 182, 184, 185
APES, 63, 64, 65, 122, 146, 162
Approximation (to Open Texture), 29, 30, 32,
157
Argument, Argumentation, 15, 18, 21, 22, 23,
24, 33, 35, 38, 40, 41, 45, 56, 68, 73, 78,

CABARET, 34, 82, 98, 122, 140
Case-Based Computer System, 33, 41, 94,
100, 112, 122, 177
Case-Based Reasoning, 32, 33, 41, 56, 57,
80, 82, 94, 98, 111, 111, 115, 123, 128, 130,
131, 136, 137, 140, 141, 143, 144, 165, 169,
180, 191, 194, 197
Cases,
    fictious, *See* hypothetical
    hypothetical, 38, 69, 70, 84, 85, 86,
    95, 98, 103, 104, 105, 106, 129, 131,
    136, 138, 141, 145, 174, 176, 194,
    195
    imaginary, *See* hypothetical
    matching, 96, 97, 128, 135
    previous, 13, 17,18, 23,24, 25, 26,
    29, 40, 41, 98, 99, 130, 141, 144,
    146
    See also Precedents
    representation of, 127, 128, 129, 131
Case Law, 13-17, 23, 26, 27, 28, 33, 34, 40,